A WAY FORWARD

Why younger generations are leaving churches,
and the art of being interested vs. interesting

Caleb Foss

Foss, 2023

A WAY FORWARD

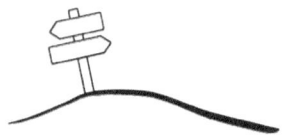

Written and Published by Caleb Foss

Edited by Geoff Heald

Hayden, ID

E-Book ISBN: 979-8-9895933-0-9

Paperback ISBN: 979-8-9895933-1-6

Hardcover ISBN: 979-8-9895933-2-3

The names of many characters and certain story details have been changed to protect the privacy of those involved.

CONTENTS

INTRODUCTION

When I'm honest, I don't consider myself to be particularly wise. Sure, I have those times when I feel like I am God's gift to the people around me. (I regularly remind my wife how lucky she is...just in case she was to forget.) However, those are usually followed shortly thereafter by some sort of deeply humbling experience that reminds me of how much I have to learn. Even now as I write, I ask myself, "What makes me arrogant enough to think that someone else would want to read this?" I don't have a great answer to that question. What I do have is a frustration at how Christianity is failing to impact teens and young adults, combined with a deep desire to see them truly experience the joy and freedom a life with Christ can bring. This has been my inspiration to learn more about the process of adolescence and how it affects the Christian experience.

I have been working in youth and young adult ministry in some form for more than two decades, which mostly just means I am getting old. (Though my wife still asks me on a regular basis if I'm 12 years old, so that has to count for something.) During this time, I have learned much from others, made many mistakes, and experienced moments of growth and clarity that have helped develop my ministry. I have had the chance to learn, through my own study and occasionally in person, from some truly great pioneers in youth ministry. The research and writing done by the likes of Kara Powell, Doug Fields, Chap Clark, Jake Mulder, Brad Griffin, and others connected with Youth Specialties and the Fuller Youth Research Center have contributed to the foundation upon which my beliefs regarding ministry have grown. Books such as *Growing Young, Growing With*, and most recently *3 Big Questions That Change Every Teenager: Making the Most of Your Conversations and Connections* are filled with valuable information to help individuals and churches learn to be successful in youth and young adult ministry.

So why write another book? Because things aren't changing. Many if not most of the friends I grew up with are no longer involved in church. In the more than twenty years that I have been working with youth and young adults, there has been little improvement. The Christian Church has arguably grown worse at reaching these communities. My own faith community struggles to have an impact. There are too many churches where this 40+ year old (who internally is twelve, mind you) would be the youngest in attendance. Challenging social and political issues threaten to make things even more difficult over the next few years.

The good news is, we have a way forward. The gospel, when applied, still has the power to actually change lives and communities. Ministry is much less complicated than we often make it out to be. However, it doesn't happen by accident. Unless we take intentional steps to connect with youth and young adults, becoming a part of their story, we will continue to struggle.

Many of the stories I share are from my own experience. It is the lens through which I see and process the world around me. As I share these parts of my journey, I hope to be another voice in the conversation, calling all of us to truly experience love and grace in our own lives, and then letting that love and grace spill over into the lives of the people around us.

THREE STORIES

The Road Trip

"Honestly, all I really want to do next year is go on a giant road trip."

I was nearing the end of my freshman year in college, and my buddy Ben and I were driving back from Ridge-to-River, a race in Wenatchee, WA that combined cross-country skiing, down-hill skiing, biking, running, and canoeing. We had put together a dream team of college friends that had placed second in the prestigious Recreational Church Division, earning us a shiny second place trophy. (Never mind that there was only one other team in our division.) The trip had sparked an already smolder-ing desire for adventure, and on our way home Ben and I had both confided in each other that we really didn't feel like going to school the next year. We both had friends who were going to various locations around the globe as student missionaries but none of those options had really piqued our interest. His statement started the wheels in our minds turning.

Over the next couple hours we developed our plan. I would call schools around the United States and Canada with an offer to come as Week of Prayer speakers. That way they could pay for our gas, feed us and give us places to stay. We could find someone to donate a bus or some sort of old vehicle, which Ben could fix as he had recently earned an Associate's Degree in Automotive Technology, that could be used to transport us and a few more of our friends on our adventure. All we had to do was to get the Student Mission's Department at Walla Walla College (now Walla Walla University) to endorse our plan to give us some credibility, and we would be set.

Amazingly, our meeting with the Student Missions Director resulted in a tentative "yes". We could say we were from Walla Walla College, while at the same time they could maintain some plausible deniability if things went down in flames. We set about putting together a team of people who we thought could be ministry assets, and quite frankly would be fun to hang out with, and I began making contacts. Our schedule filled rapidly, we procured a 15-passenger van from a friend's dad, and in September of 2000 Operation: Live the Life hit the road.

Over the next year our team of ten traveled over 30k miles, spoke at 30+ different schools, churches, and even a hospital, and had the time of our lives. Ben put his degree to work fixing the van, which would occasionally catch on fire, required a transmission overhaul on the side of the road, and had the axle fall out on at least one occasion. Through our travels we experienced what we believe were instances where God interacted with us in very tangible ways. We were dependent on miracles, and were blessed despite our youthful, blissful ignorance.

At one point following a week at Highland Academy in Tennessee, we had a week with nothing scheduled. Three of us joined a friend who lived nearby for a week-long trip to Coco Beach, Florida in his bright red Mustang Saleen for a surf adventure. We arrived after dark with no money for lodging. Eventually we discovered a quiet field near Cape Canaveral and tossed our sleeping bags out in the grass. The next morning, we were greeted by a space shuttle launch over our heads and about twenty kids at a nearby school bus stop we had unwittingly set up camp next to. We spent the week learning to surf and amusing ourselves at the wary response from the parents who accompanied their kids to the bus stop and couldn't stop staring at the four scruffy squatters with a fancy sports car sleeping in the field nearby.

When the weekend arrived, we decided to perform a social experiment which involved attending one of the local churches and seeing how they responded to our shaggy crew. We stopped by the local McDonalds to "freshen up" in the bathroom and selected a church in the area. None of us had brought any type of dress attire and we arrived with matted hair, t-shirts, board shorts, and flip-flops.

The service was already underway when we walked in the front door, and no one was in the lobby to greet us. Upon opening the next set of double doors we found ourselves standing in the center aisle at the back of a very full worship center. The room was filled with gray hair, fancy dresses, and three-piece suits. As it happened, our entry coincided with the end of opening prayer and, as if on cue, every head turned to look, and then to stare at the newcomers at the back of the room. The only empty seats were on the front row, and we gleefully, in the name of science, walked down and planted our boardshort-covered behinds right in front of the pastor.

During the service It was hard to tell exactly what the response behind us was without being too conspicuous, so we had to wait till the end to truly assess our impact on the local congregation. Small groups of dignified men and women huddled together, casting occasional glances in our direction as we stood in the lobby. Eventually a group sent a couple emissaries to engage us in awkward conversation. Once they found out that we were there on a surf trip, they found what seemed to be the one youngish person in attendance who apparently had at least some experience surfing to pass us off to. After some time in awkward, though not unpleasant conversation with our new surf "buddy", most of the people cleared out, and the pastor invited us home for lunch. We shared our story, including the part about us sleeping in the grass of a nearby field, which prompted a few awkward jokes from the pastor's wife about smoking "grass", and otherwise enjoyed a nice, non-fast-food meal, accompanied by some educational thoughts regarding the dangers of eating food from a tin can, before heading back to our home next to the bus stop.

As we debriefed later, our thoughts were mixed. A couple of people had stepped out of their comfort zone to engage us and had at least attempted to put us in contact with someone who might be able to connect with us over surfing. However, it was also apparent that we made them nervous, and our interactions were uncomfortable. We were seen as a mission project that required courage and determination to complete. The vast majority, after eyeing us as we walked down the center aisle during the service, did their best to ignore us. It was clear that we didn't belong. For us, it was fun because it was an experiment. However, I can say that if we had been looking for something more, we would have been disappointed. None of us would have returned.

Anonymous

I am part of what I consider to be an extraordinary church. My wife told me after we had been attending for about a year that it was the first church she had ever gone to because she liked it and it made a difference in her life, not because she was supposed to. We have an incredible community of friends, and we feel like we can be ourselves there, which is hard to come by for those who have worked in the pastoral industry.

It is the kind of place that I will frequently invite people to visit. I don't do it because I feel guilty, it isn't something that I'm "supposed" to do. I do it because I want others to feel the connection that I feel when I am there. Earlier this year I invited a young couple that I had been working with for a few weeks to come visit. I wanted them to feel the same love and grace that I had experienced when I began attending.

Following their visit, I was eager to hear more about their experience. At first, they danced around the question, telling me about how they appreciated parts of the sermon, etc. Finally, with a bit more prodding, they indicated that they had actually been a bit disappointed. Apparently, besides me, no one had talked to them while they were there. Now, to be fair, they had made a somewhat hurried exit after the service was over, but in the end, they still came away disappointed. No one engaged them. No one reached out and sought to connect with them. (Other than me...I don't count.) No one learned their story. While they were present, they weren't seen.

Was it an off day for our crew? Sure. There are likely some legitimate reasons why, but ultimately none of that mattered to them. In a place where I experience a profound sense of belonging, they left feeling anonymous, alone, and unvalued .

A Safe Place

I couldn't believe the words I was reading in the Facebook message I had just received. "Joshua is dead." Over the next few days the story unfolded. He had been out riding his Gsx-R 750 "crotch rocket" motorcycle, which was a newfound obsession for him in the year since I had moved away. He had been hanging out with some friends and was on his way home when a local police officer tried to pull him over for speeding. Joshua was 20, invincible, and decided to make a run for it. Sadly, as a relatively new rider, his skill level didn't match his ambition and courage. Trying to elude his pursuers, he lost control while attempting to turn into a residential neighborhood and the resulting crash ended his life.

I first heard about Josh shortly after beginning a new job as a youth pastor. "Good luck!" an informant told me. "All he wants to do is argue. It's exhausting." Over the next four years Josh became an established part of our youth group. He did ask a lot of questions. However, what others identified as an argumentative spirit was actually a deep desire to know what was true in life and a commitment to not accept inadequate answers. He wasn't willing to accept explanations based on tradition or what he perceived as irrational reasoning. Adult volunteers were scared of him at times because there was a reasonable chance they were going to get questions that they couldn't address to his satisfaction. They might not have the right answer.

Josh and I had many amazing conversations about life and faith. I didn't always have answers. There were times when I had to admit I didn't know. There were times when his questions, or blunt responses to others could be frustrating. But once I got past the surface and we learned to trust each other, I discovered that there was so much more to Josh than the picture that was painted for me when I first arrived. He was not a bad kid. He was incredibly loyal and cared deeply for his friends. He attended our events regularly and frequently helped as we sought ways to serve in our community.

I get just a bit misty eyed even now as I think about flying down for his memorial service. I don't remember many details from that trip, nor the part that I played in his memorial. What I do remember is a conversation with his mom and brother after the service. She attended another church in town that wasn't a part of our faith community, but through Joshua's involvement we had been able to interact a number of times. With tears in her eyes, she thanked me for being a part of Josh's life. She went on to tell me how my acceptance and friendship had created one of the few positive interactions with religion that Josh had experienced. She was so thankful that he had discovered a safe place to learn about himself and about God's love for him.

Points to Ponder

1. Have you ever felt like you didn't fit within a religious community? What made you feel that way?

2. Have you ever felt alone or unseen, whether within your faith community or one you were visiting? What emotions did that produce? What did you do to deal with the situation?

3. Do you feel like your religious community is safe for teens and young adults? Why or why not?

4. Do you feel safe within your religious community? Why or why not?

5. If you could change something about your religious community to make it a place that was safe for teens and young adults, what would it be?

Awesome for Jesus

In 2004 I underwent many of the major changes in life one can experience.

1. I graduated from Walla Walla College (Now Walla Walla University)

2. Married my fiancé (Now my wife)

3. Sold my car without air conditioning and purchased another with it

4. Purchased my first cell phone (A flip phone, which I promptly smashed while casually riding my skateboard with my hands in my pockets and hitting a rock.)

    5. Moved to California

    6. Started my career as a youth pastor.

One of the first things that the head pastor told me in our first meeting was, "You need to be 'The Guy'." Apparently there had been some friction amongst the youth leaders prior to my involvement, and he felt that they needed some strong leadership. In fact, one of the more involved leaders had applied for the job and had been turned down. (No awkwardness there for a freshly graduated 24-year-old!) He felt the best strategy was for me to take over all the ministry for a bit to avoid an elongated power struggle. I would need to be the one to teach the high school program every week. I would be the one to make the plans and build connections. I would be the one to draw all the teens together.

Growing up I had inhabited a strange space in my religious community. My family was fairly prominent in our church and for us kids, ministry started at a young age. When I was two years old, I began a prestigious singing career and within a few years we began traveling to different churches around the northwest to put on worship services. My parents used the acronym REKINDLE, though I can't remember what each letter stood for. Each family member would sing songs and deliver speaking parts that went along with the theme. As my brothers and I grew and developed, so did our production. My older brother was the star vocalist and took care of most of the solo parts. For my younger brother and me, my dad created robot suits from cardboard boxes and aluminum foil that we proudly wore for one of the songs. This was our time to shine. I can still remember one time when we went to a church that had a spotlight. It didn't take me long to realize that I could control the reflection off my shiny, state of the art, 1986 robot costume and direct it at various members of the audience. It was delightful to watch them grimace, squint, cover their eyes and try to squirm out of the light. I could tell they loved it.

As I grew into my adolescent years, I outgrew my robot costume and found that it was much easier to be "cool" if I wore baggy pants and played the guitar instead of just singing. As my skills improved, I began to learn that worship songs actually existed outside of the hymnal and old song books that I had been exposed to. I also learned that I could incorporate guitar riffs from bands like Smashing Pumpkins, Metallica, etc. and make worship "cool" instead of something weird that I was embarrassed to be a part of in front of my friends. I had been taught from a young age to let my light shine, but that didn't mean things had to be dull or boring. As I progressed through high school, I became one of the spiritual leaders at Upper Columbia Academy. When I graduated, I began working at Camp Mivoden, and also interned as a youth pastor at my home church during the summer. In all these situations my mission was the same. Show my peers, and then youth that you could be cool and love Jesus too. By the time I started my job in California, I had been doing "youth ministry" for years.

In addition to my spiritual life, I had developed a number of skills that helped me distinguish myself socially. I was a pretty good athlete and as I moved through high school and college, I began competing and picked up some sponsors as a wakeboarder and freestyle skier. I also continued to progress as a musician and began writing my own songs. Additionally, I found that I could use sarcasm and humor to appear smooth and confident. Growing up I had been taught that anything you do can be done for the glory of God. I had aspirations of becoming a professional skier or wakeboarder and using this platform to spread the gospel. Even though I never achieved pro status, I understood that these and other tools could be powerful.

As my journey continued, I noticed that many of the people I knew and interacted with really weren't interested in spirituality. Many of the "cool people" didn't find religion that interesting. Through the combination of these circumstances, I was taught that it was my role to be Awesome for Jesus...Something I felt like the head pastor confirmed when I arrived at my first pastoring job.

And to be honest I was reasonably good at it. If you were a jock, I had both the team sports and extreme sports covered. If you were a musician, I played music in church and also played in an obscure punk/alternative/metal band. I was the funny guy and made church entertaining. If you were a skeptic, we could have conversations that other adults were too afraid to have. If you were obnoxious, I could light you up with wit and sarcasm. We did mission trips, ski trips, surf trips, etc. I made Christianity cool again.

Our youth group grew rapidly. We began to have kids from other local churches coming to our events, which terrified other local pastors. A number of churches in the area hired their own youth pastors to try to compete. Some pastors even forbade their youth and youth leaders to have anything to do with us for fear that they would want to attend our church instead. Some began to spread rumors about what we did to make parents afraid to let their kids attend.

Our programming was robust and diverse. We took the high school and college students on mission trips to Mexico, where they built houses for families that needed a place to live, and also ran a kid's program at a local church. We took ski trips to Tahoe and surf trips to Santa Cruz. In addition to our weekly youth group meetings, we also had a Friday night Bible study and student leadership team that met every week. I attended football and basketball games, cheerleading competitions, drama productions, graduations, birthday parties, etc. I visited high school and college campuses, and regularly invited those in our group to meet me at Chipotle for a burrito so I could listen to their story.

After four years of successful ministry, I was done! My wife was done! Four years of being "Awesome for Jesus" had all but killed us.

Points to Ponder

1. In what ways have you sought in your life to be "Awesome for Jesus?"

2. What are the benefits from this type of ministry? What are the challenges it creates?

3. Have you struggled with burnout in ministry? If so, where did it come from? How did you manage it? Was your method of management successful?

4. What do you believe causes us to sacrifice our health and relationships for ministry?

5. What are some other pursuits that cause us to sacrifice our health and relationships? In what ways are these similar to the pursuit of ministry? In what ways are they different?

THE EXODUS

Churches in North America are facing a crisis. Youth and young adults are leaving Christianity in alarming numbers. Within my own faith community, there are many churches that are completely devoid of young members. According to a study done by Lifeway Research in 2017[1], approximately two-thirds of Protestant Christian young adults quit attending church regularly after graduating from high school. Of those who quit, 29% reported that they planned to leave after graduation. This means that for approximately 70% of them leaving was not an intentional decision. Apparently for them, it wasn't that they were angry at church, they were just indifferent. Church hadn't made a significant enough impact in their lives to inspire them to stay.

According to the Lifeway study, nearly all of those who dropped out noted a change in their life situation as a reason they quit attending. The following chart illustrates the top five reasons that they moved on. (Survey participants could list more than one.) As I look at their answers, moving to college or a change in work responsibilities were significant factors in discontinued church attendance. For others there was some sort of feeling of disconnect or disagreement on an issue that was the catalyst for their departure. However, the interesting and disturbing thing is that fewer than one-third of those who left reported that they had actually planned on taking a break from church when they graduated from high school. Leaving wasn't an intentional decision.

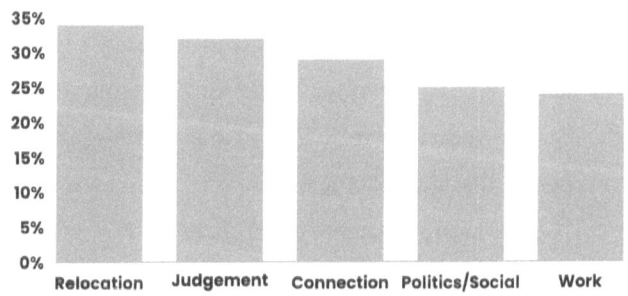

TOP 5 REASONS FOR LEAVING

Among young adults (ages 23-30) who attended a Protestant church regularly for at least a year in high school. Data obtained from www.lifewayresearch.com.

Relocation: They moved and never got around to finding another church.

Judgment: They felt judged by their faith community.

Connection: They felt disconnected from their faith community.

Politics/Social: Their faith community embraced different political or social ideas.

Work: They were just too busy at work or their schedule didn't line up with that of their faith community.

Ben Trueblood, who is the Director of Student Ministry at Lifeway describes it this way. "For the most part, people aren't leaving the church out of bitterness, the influence of college atheists, or a renunciation of their faith...What the research tells us may be even more concerning for Protestant churches: there was nothing about the church experience or faith foundation of those teenagers that caused them to seek out a connection to a local church once they entered a new phase of life. The time they spent with activity in church was simply replaced by something else."[3]

In other words, Protestant churches simply aren't making a big enough difference in the lives of teens and young adults for them to choose to remain a part of the faith community. They aren't necessarily bitter or angry. They simply don't care. Elie Wiesel, a writer and Holocaust survivor once said, "The opposite of love is not hate. It is indifference."[4] If I hate something, it shows that it at least has an effect on me. If I am indifferent, it is not even worth my time to consider.

Unfortunately, this isn't a new problem. According to a Lifeway study in 2007, 70% of young adults at that time were leaving after their high school graduation. While the results indicate a slight improvement, it is not a great enough difference from their study in 2017 to be statistically significant. Other studies support the presence of this issue in the early 2000s as well. The Southern Baptist Convention reported that they were losing 70-88% after their freshman year of college.[5] Sadly, in the more than two decades since I began youth ministry little has changed.

We don't even have to look at research to know that this is happening. My friend Dave was recently telling me how most of the friends that he grew up with were no longer part of a church, with many no longer claiming to be a part of the Christian faith. He and I have similar experiences when it comes to our friends. While I have an incredible faith community that I am a part of, I can think of numerous friends and classmates that I attended Christian school with who are no longer interested in Christianity.

I believe that at least part of the reason for our lack of progress has to do with the way we have tried to deal with the problem. Churches will hire a young youth pastor, preferably as close to the teenage years as possible, so they can relate with their students. They stick them in a part of the church where they won't bother anybody and let them go nuts. Good ministry happens, teens get to know Jesus. They develop a strong connection with their youth pastor or leader. However, when they graduate from high school or the youth pastor leaves, they have no connection to anyone else. The rest of the church community has never acknowledged their existence, except for the ones who came to tell them to turn down the music during their small group time. There is nothing to anchor them in the community. Additionally, when we choose youth leaders who are close to the same age as the students, they have significantly less life experience and are less likely to have established a healthy identity. Without adequate mentorship, this can lead to mistakes that those with more life experience and a more fully developed sense of their own identity will be less likely to make.

I don't want to diminish the role of the youth pastor or youth leader. People in these positions have the ability to profoundly impact the teens and young adults that they work with. However, if this is our only strategy, we will continue to struggle to connect younger generations to our faith communities.

This model of youth ministry has another byproduct that is also concerning. Youth Pastor/Youth Leader burnout. Youth leaders tend to shoulder the entire weight of ministry while their churches applaud and validate them. While the organization may be very supportive financially, the responsibility for building relational connections is left to just a few. A study in the *Journal of Psychology and Theology* published in 2018 looked at relational capacity and how it affects those in youth ministry. The average person has about 150 people in their social network, 15 close friends, and 5 deep friendships. This is considered our relational capacity. However, when researchers looked at ministers, and more specifically those involved in youth ministry, they tend to have a smaller social network (120 people) but more close relationships (25) and best friends (9).[6] According to Caleb Roose, an author and project manager at the Fuller Youth Institute, "youth ministers tend to have bloated inner circles but a smaller number of overall friends...While maintaining relationships with best friends has been shown to guard against burnout, sustaining more than 15 close relationships actually significantly increases the risk of burnout. Keeping up with a large inner circle eventually wears on us."[7] Ultimately, the youth ministry will either top out when the leaders reach their effective relational capacity, or the leaders will burn out, or both.

When we look biblically, this is a concept that Jesus seems to have understood. He chose 12 disciples with which he developed a close relationship, three of which became his closest friends. While he preached to large crowds, he kept his close relationships to a select few. On this scale he was able to influence them in such a way that, when he was gone, they were able to continue the movement and change the world. When we leave just a few youth leaders to minister to a large number of kids, we diminish their impact and jeopardize their mental wellbeing.

It probably isn't a news flash for most of us that young adults are leaving the church. However, the scale at which it happens is certainly concerning. The potential for that number to increase even more in the future is concerning as well. One small redeeming factor is that of the 2/3 that are leaving, approximately 1/3 of that group do return.[8] However, even with those who do return in their 30s or 40s, we have missed out on a decade or two of their involvement in our community. Their voices, energy, perspective, and potential to spread love and grace are lost during that time. It is our loss.

Points to Ponder

1. Do you have any personal examples of young adults leaving your faith community? What factors do you feel contributed to them leaving?

2. Has your faith community taken any steps to try and incorporate teens and young adults? What are they? What has gone well? What needs to be improved on?

3. Do you feel like your faith community has enough volunteers to adequately connect relationally with teens and young adults? What are some of the barriers for

volunteers?

4. Have you at any point left your faith community? If so, why? If you never have, what has caused you to stay?

ADOLESCENT ABANDONMENT

Not long after I began working as a youth pastor in California, I attended a youth leader training conference in San Diego hosted by Youth Specialties. I didn't want to go initially. After all, I had been doing ministry for years in the camp setting, and to be honest I was underwhelmed by "training" events I had been a part of in the past. However, the head pastor in his wisdom strongly encouraged my wife Calista and me to go. Before long I had run out of excuses and signed up.

To make a long story short, the conference blew my mind. On the first night more than 5,000 youth leaders gathered together in the venue. The energy was palpable as we waited for things to get underway. Following a creative and humorous video to get people warmed up we were instructed to look underneath our chairs where we each discovered a rubber band powered foam rocket. For the next five minutes absolute chaos ensued as 5,000 foam rockets were lobbed around the room. There was no one to tell us to turn the music down. No one to tell us to stop before someone lost an eye. It was beautiful. I had never been around that many people excited about working with teenagers. The speakers were incredible, offering encouragement and wisdom to all of us youth leaders from their years of research and experience. We worshiped with the likes of a young Phil Whickham and Hawk Nelson (now I'm just dating myself). The breakout sessions were filled with useful information and while I still had much to learn, I left the event with a new perspective on what youth ministry could be.

Of the many positive experiences I had during that weekend, there was one breakout session that stood out to me and ultimately laid the foundation for my ministry to youth and young adults. I don't remember who the teacher was, but the session dealt with understanding youth culture. It was based on information from studies and research that had been done by the Fuller Youth Institute. (Since that time, they have written about their continued research in books such as *Growing Young* and *Growing With*, and more recently *3 Big Questions That Change Every Teenager: Making the Most of Your Conversations and Connections*. I recommend that anyone involved in youth and young adult ministry take a look at these books. They are excellent resources.) It gave me a window into the process of adolescence and the need for relational connection. The framework this class created has stuck with me as I have continued on my ministry journey.

Changes in the Process of Adolescence

In order to know how to approach ministry to youth and young adults, we must first understand more about the process of adolescence. This is a process that is always changing and evolving as our society evolves, but there are some core principles that always stay the same. When researchers looked at the process of adolescence over the last century, they first had to come up with a working definition that could be applied both historically and in the present. In the end they decided to define the start of adolescence as when children or teens first begin to experience the biological changes associated with beginning puberty. This could be tracked historically.

The completion of adolescence is a little tougher to define. According to Chap Clark at the Fuller Youth Institute, "The problem is that when a culture (like ours) lacks rites of passage designed to prepare and train young people for adulthood, and then removes almost every definable ritual signpost from childhood to adulthood, it's very difficult to agree on when adolescence ends and adulthood begins."[1] He states that there are two broad assumptions that define the transition to adulthood in our culture today.

1. I know and am fairly comfortable with who I am.

2. I am willing to take responsibility for myself.

In the book *3 Big Questions That Shape Your Future*[2], which is based on research performed by the Fuller Youth Institute, the authors suggest that there are essentially three primary questions that are universal to the adolescent experience.

1. Who am I? (Question of **Identity**)

2. Where do I fit? (Question of **Belonging**)

3. What difference do I make? (Question of **Autonomy)**

When I think about these three questions, they are an expansion of the first assumption mentioned by Chap Clark above. Completion of adolescence hinges on individuals being able to answer these three questions in a satisfactory manner and taking responsibility for themselves.

If you look at how the process of growing up has changed over the last century, an interesting pattern emerges. In 1997 a pediatrician named Marcia Herman-Giddens published a study with the American Academy of Pediatrics that indicated the average age for the onset of puberty was declining. (Most studies have looked at females because there is more data available.) In the pre-1900s the process of adolescence began on average at 16.6 years of age. [3] In 1920, it had decreased to 14.6 years of age. In 1980 it had decreased further to 12.5 years old. Similar sets of figures have been reported for boys, albeit with a delay of around a year. Most of the studies that indicate this decrease in average age are based on the development of breast tissue. Studies I was able to find regarding the onset of menstruation were a bit more mixed. However, an article in Scientific American reported the current age of onset at 12, versus 14 a century ago. [4]

So what is the process like now? A study by JAMA Pediatrics published in 2020 [5] puts the median age of when adolescence begins in the United States somewhere between 8.8-10.3 based on their region. Generally, this age has decreased about 3 months per decade since the 1970's.

In contrast, the end point for this adolescent period has also been changing. By the time our great grandparents were in their late teens and early twenties, many had answered the three questions. Many of them were married, had started an occupation, begun a family, etc. In the 1920s around 8% of boys aged 10-15 were already working. [6] When the age range was expanded to 19, over 50% of boys had entered the workforce. [7] The number jumps to around 90% for men in their early 20s. There was a significant portion of the population that was already on their career path by the time they hit age 20. These numbers coincide with lower rates of those continuing their education past high school, or even grade school in some cases.

Young adults also tended to get married earlier. According to a Pew Research article in 2010 the median age in 1960 was 20.3 for women and 22.8 for men.[8] These numbers climbed to 26.5 and 28.7 in 2010, with only 51% of adults over the age of 18 being married vs 72% in 1960. A more recent article by Bowling Green State University reported that in 2021 the median age at first marriage had increased to 28.6 for women and 30.4 for men.[9]

And what about just taking responsibility for oneself in general? A study in *The Lancet* in 2018[10] proposed that age 24 was actually a better age based on societal norms for adopting adult roles and responsibilities. They noted the average age for young adults to leave home was 25. However, it is not uncommon for people at this age to still be struggling with life direction and purpose, which makes taking responsibility for one's life difficult. If we define the end of adolescence as having answered the questions of identity, belonging, autonomy, and self-responsibility, these can frequently stretch through the 20's and beyond.

The bottom line is, what used to be primarily a process of the teenage years is now stretched out over a couple decades with a less certain end point. Add to this the busyness created by societal pressure to maximize involvement in sports, academics, clubs, etc., and it leads to what the authors of *Growing Young* call "Pervasive Stress".[11] As the process of adolescence begins at a younger age, so does the stress associated with these changes. Add to this the increasing difficulty with answering questions regarding identity, autonomy, and belonging and it creates an underlying stress that frequently extends for more than a decade.

I want to take a moment here to also discuss societal stressors as well. As I write this paragraph, we are approximately three years since the start of the COVID-19 pandemic. The Center for Disease Control indicated that young adults were nearly three times more likely to experience anxiety and depression in 2021[12] than they were in 2019[13] before the pandemic began. Even in 2023 rates of anxiety and depression remain high at around 46%. War is raging in the Ukraine and multiple other parts of the globe. Our political climate is more divisive than it has been in decades. There is uncertainty regarding the economy and the job market. Many Christians are taking a look at the world around them and wondering if this is the time Jesus spoke of when he talked about the end of the world. Pile all of this on top of the inherent stress of going through adolescence, and it has created an epidemic of mental health disorders.

I work at a summer camp in Northern Idaho called Camp MiVoden. One of my job titles there is that of Staff Mentor. Throughout the summer there is a steady stream of young adults coming to my office for support as they process life. I am honored to be a part of their journey, and it is an amazing privilege for me to be able to join them in this part of their story. However, I am also reminded on a daily basis how much these young adults feel all of these stressors. They need the support of their Christian community as they go through this part of their journey.

Sadly, the places where in previous decades teens and young adults were able to find support have become less dependable. For millennia the *Family* was the primary means of guidance and support for people going through the process of adolescence. While it has never been perfect, it still functioned adequately enough in most instances to provide a basic level of training and support. However, without even looking at research, most people will recognize that families are often broken. 1 in 4 marriages end in divorce.[14] (The adage that 50% of marriages don't make it is false. But 25% is still a lot, and those who marry again are much more likely to experience another divorce.) The number of people physically, mentally, emotionally, and sexually abused within their families is astounding. 1 in 4 women and 1 in 9 men suffer severe domestic violence.[15] 1 in 5 women have been raped, 1 in 10 by an intimate partner. Even in families where none of this takes place, parents frequently don't have time to spend with their children. There is an epidemic of busyness that limits meaningful interactions within families. Even when they are together, many families struggle to communicate effectively.

Beyond the family, society has developed a number of other mechanisms for helping teens and young adults through this process. The education system can be a source of identity, value, and ultimately autonomy. However, it also struggles in many places to adequately address the needs of the students. Furthermore, it tends to reinforce the idea that your value is based on your ability to produce good grades, go to a good college, etc. For those who don't perform well in the current school system, it can actually teach them that they aren't valuable and that they don't belong. Clubs and sports teams can provide a sense of belonging and teach some life skills. They also can reinforce the idea that in order to be valuable a person one must win at all costs and exclude the losers. Then there are less healthy places where adolescents search for answers, such as cliques, gangs, etc. In many ways, society has abandoned these people to figure things out on their own.

And then we have the church. This is the place where teens and young adults are supposed to be able to find answers to these questions. We try to fill the void. The challenge is that the church is full of broken people. Many of the older members are still trying to find answers to the same three questions (Who am I? Where do I belong? and Do I matter?) themselves. Instead of youth and young adult ministry being about the adolescents it is meant to help, it often becomes more about the adults who are doing it. (More on this later!) When decisions are made that impact multiple generations, many people tend to focus on protecting what is theirs as opposed to looking for a cross-generational solution. For those who are willing to venture into the adolescent realm, it is often terrifying. There is an interesting phenomenon that I've observed when many youth leaders walk into a room full of teenagers. Instantly many of the insecurities they had when they were in high school return. They tend to gravitate towards certain people in the program that they feel will accept them more. They revert to many of the same strategies they used when they were younger to try to establish their value within the group. It's like they are back in high school again, which for some was traumatizing the first time they were there.

Churches who want to have an effective youth ministry will frequently seek to hire youth pastors and staff. Those who can't afford it are forced to find a lay leader who is up for the challenge. These brave souls engage themselves in ministry while the general population of the church does their best not to make eye contact with the youth and young adults who attend their program. In some cases, churches will just give up altogether and resign themselves to being a dying community.

The common thread through all of these scenarios is a generation of adolescents who are left to find their path to adulthood on their own. When a teen or young adult asks "Who am I?", the answer from many Christian communities is "Not who you should be." When they ask, "Where do I belong?" the answer is, "Not here." And when they ask, "Do I matter?" the answer is, "Only when I talk about attendance numbers or the future of my church." Yet we continue to wonder why young adults are leaving. Even in a church like my own where we serve breakfast, have a great youth pastor, focus on having a less dated worship style, and use cool videos in our worship service, we will struggle to maintain youth and young adults in our community unless we make an intentional effort to build cross-generational connections.

The Role of Technology

First, let it be known that I am not a technology hater. I use my phone and computer for talking, texting, browsing the internet, and social media on a daily basis. It's great and has been an invaluable resource when it comes to maintaining my supply of "dad" jokes. However, it is important for us to recognize the effect that social media and technology in general has had on our society.

Gen Z (People born in the 1990s and early 2000s) is currently being referred to by many as "the loneliest generation". Our world has shrunk as the role of technology has grown. It is now possible for us to communicate with thousands of people around the globe with a single post. However, as Ryan Jenkins wrote in *Psychology Today*, technology also has the ability to create barriers to connection. Jenkins noted that there were three ways that technology is contributing to social isolation.[16]

Overstimulation: We live in a "plugged in" world, which ironically uses very few wires these days. We are constantly preoccupied and distracted. In addition to the normal business of life with work, school, chores, family logistics, etc., we also have constant access to information. Smartphones have allowed us to maintain "connectedness" almost anywhere, but this connection to data frequently acts as a barrier to connecting with real people. When we do communicate, it is often through email, DM (Direct Messaging), and other means that are devoid of direct human interaction and often lack empathy. Our world lacks margin, space where we can spend unstructured time together. It is in this space that relationships are made.

Social Media: According to Jenkins, there are a number of studies that show heavy social media use significantly increases loneliness. Because it is also possible for us to exert a lot of control over what we reveal about ourselves to others, we create the identity we think people want to see, while comparing our true selves to the identities that others create. He quotes Roger Patulny, an associate professor of sociology at the University of Wollongong (best university name ever) in Australia in saying the following, "Social media is most effective in tackling loneliness when it is used to enhance existing relationships or forge new meaningful connections. On the other hand, it is counterproductive if used as a substitute for real-life social interaction. Thus, it is not social media itself, but the way we integrate it into our existing lives which impacts loneliness."[17]

Remember the study I mentioned earlier that looked at the number of friends an average person has? Social media has drastically increased the number of surface level friends and acquaintances with whom we share select information. However, quantity is not a substitution for quality. The tendency now is for us to be known at a surface level with a manufactured identity by many, instead of truly being known at a deep level by a smaller number of people. Our ability to build meaningful relationships is stunted.

Dependency Shift: Jenkins third barrier to connection was the change in how we learn about new things. Information used to be primarily obtained through other people. In ancient cultures, you learned about the world and your place in it from other individuals in the community. Even a few decades ago, if you needed to fix your car you talked to a mechanic. If you needed to fix your sink, you called a plumber. You talked to a real person. Until recently, the passing on of information was a primary connection point between generations. Moms and dads, grandpas and grandmas would connect with younger generations as they changed tires, cooked meals, etc. Today, our primary sources of information come from technology. I can diagnose the problem with my car, find and purchase the needed parts, and learn how to complete the repair all without actually talking to a person. While this is incredibly handy, it also decreases the number of connection points we have with other people.

Social media has also had a significant effect on how young adults and teens process their own identity. Self-censorship allows users to heavily control the way they are perceived by the rest of the world. Frequently users have multiple identities that they use as they interact with different groups of people. I was recently chatting with a friend who illustrates this well. When I went to connect with him on social media, I ended up running into two different accounts. Unsure if one was a fake and wanting to know how best to communicate with him, I asked about the two. He works in the outdoor and construction industries, and also is very involved in his local church. He told me that one identity is the one that is "safe" to share with his "church" friends. The other is the one that he will use with his "secular" friends. Generally, this works well, until he encounters someone like me who interacts with him in both worlds. This can lead to confusion.

My friend is in his 50's and therefore has an understanding of who he is that was developed long before social media existed. However, for teens and young adults working to understand who they are in the midst of a social media dominated world, things can get confusing. Instead of having a central identity that they process the world from, I am worried that adolescents now more than ever are torn between multiple identities. These don't seem to be different iterations of the same root identity. It is as if they are truly trying to live multiple lives simultaneously. In *Growing Young* the authors refer to an "Identity Lockbox" where things like religion, politics, race, gender, class, etc., identities are locked away from the rest of the world.[18] The downside is that while they are making decisions about their identity and how to express it, these values are locked away and don't necessarily impact their decision-making in other contexts.

Another way social media affects the development of one's identity is through the algorithms that are used to connect people in the various networks. These algorithms are created to connect people with similar ideas, beliefs, and interests. This means that if I like surfing, which I do, it is going to connect me with other surfers. The byproduct of this is that we end up being connected almost exclusively with people who think like us. We encounter fewer new ideas, and there are fewer people to hold us accountable if we become imbalanced in some way. We tend to interact with our homogeneous community and think that the rest of the world must think like this as well. Some of the rough edges that might be worn off as we interact with a diverse community are reinforced and "sharpened".

Older Generations Have Lost Their Voice

Because older generations have essentially left adolescents to figure things out on their own, they have lost their voice with this community. The "generation gap" continues to widen. The session that I attended nearly twenty years ago called it the "creation of a world beneath." Essentially these younger generations have created their own world that adult generations have very little influence in. When there are questions about life, spirituality, relationships, sex, drugs, mental illness, etc., they will turn to their peers or their online community instead of interacting with older generations who possess more life experience. This trend has continued over the last few decades, turning the generation gap into more of a chasm.

Growing up in our society is challenging. Adolescents are being faced with complexities, conflicting ideas, and unrest that previous generations didn't experience in the same way or to the same extent. This doesn't mean that previous generations had it easy, but it does mean that we need to recognize the effect that these factors have on the teens and young adults that we interact with. Unfortunately, in many if not most cases, the Christian church has failed to recognize these factors and has failed to connect with a large percentage of people going through adolescence. There is a hole in many of our church communities. The reality is, if we don't adapt, our churches will be left behind. God is at work regardless of what we do. However, we may miss out on our opportunity to be a part of what He is doing with younger generations.

Pop Quiz:

> 1. *When was the last time you spoke to a youth or young adult in your church that you didn't already know?*

> 2. *How many names of youth/young adults in your church do you know?*

3. *Of the ones that you do know, what do you know of their story?*

Forgotten

When I was 6 years old, I saved the day. Our family lived in the small town of Morton, Washington where my dad was the teacher/principal of a one room school. I think there were nine kids total from grades 1-8. My parents were also very involved in the local church. It was small, with a typical attendance of 20-30 people.

On this occasion our family was finishing up an evening music practice, and we were all tired. My grandmother had been there earlier helping us kids learn our music parts and then had headed home while my parents finished up. Finally, it was time for us to go as well. My older brother and I piled into our seats in the car while my parents locked the deadbolt on the church's front door, which required a key from both the inside and outside. They were in the vehicle with the engine running when I casually mentioned, "Are we just going to leave Ezra in there?"

My younger brother Ezra, who was probably two or three years old at the time, had fallen asleep on one of the church pews while everyone else was rehearsing, and my parents had assumed that he had gone home with my grandmother. Had I not heroically saved the day, he would have awakened to find himself alone and locked in a cold, dark church. A sure nightmare in the making. I don't believe he ever thanked me.

I think many Christian teens and young adults awaken to something similar. Suddenly they find themselves alone and "unseen" in a cold, dark church. As they strive with the complexities and stress of growing up, they find that older generations have locked up and they are alone in the dark, feeling unwanted. Church is not relevant to them because they have never really been incorporated into the community.

Points to Ponder

1. Do you feel like the teens and young adults have been adequately connected to your faith community? What has your faith community done well to connect with them? Where does it need to improve?

2. How has technology impacted how you connect with others? How do you see it impacting the people around you?

3. How have you seen questions of Identity, Autonomy, and Belonging manifested in the lives of teens and

young adults within your faith community? Has your faith community done anything to address these questions?

4. What areas do you find yourself challenged with the ideas of Identity, Autonomy, and Belonging?

5. What are some ways society puts pressure on teens and young adults? Are there ways that your faith community adds to the pressure that teens and young adults are facing? Have you asked any teens or young adults about this?

THE IDENTITY PROBLEM

I love road trips. From the yearlong adventure my friends and I embarked on in college, to the family excursions with my wife and kids, there is a freedom and exhilaration that I feel every time I hit the road. One of the things I have come to value about these trips is the time spent driving. When we were in college, Calista and I started listening to books on tape whenever we hit the road. Books on tape evolved into CDs, then MP3s, and eventually into streaming sources, but a good story never changes regardless of the medium. It's not uncommon for me to feel a twinge of disappointment when I arrive at my destination, and I have to leave my book or podcast until my next round of driving.

It was on a family surf trip to the Oregon coast in 2019 when I encountered a podcast that made a significant impression on me and the way I processed the topic of Identity. The podcast is called *Freakonomics*, featuring Steven Levitt, an author and professor of Economics at the University of Chicago, and John Donohue, a professor of law at Stanford Law School. They had recently published a paper entitled "The Impact of Legalized Abortion on Crime Over the Past Two Decades' which was the topic of discussion.[1] In 2001 the two of them had collaborated and presented evidence that the legalization of abortion in the early 1970s played an important role in the crime drop of the 1990s. They had also predicted that two decades from that date there would be a continued reduction in crime from what was experienced in the 1990s. This paper was the follow-up to that prediction.

In the 1990s there was suddenly a substantial drop in crime in the United States, and no one really knew why. By 1997 violent crime and property crime had fallen 30 percent, and homicide was down 40 percent.[2] Politicians and other interested parties at the time were more than happy to take credit for the phenomenon, though none of the policies enacted really could explain the change. Levitt and Donohue were intrigued and began to look for possible explanations. There was an increase in prison capacity over the two decades prior, which accounted for a percentage of the decrease, but this alone did not fully explain the change. What they noticed was that the drop in numbers coincided perfectly with when people born in the early-mid

1970s would be in their early twenties, the age when people involved in crimes tend to become more active. They then studied those years and the decades leading up to the 1990s to see what had changed, and found that this time period coincided with the Supreme Court's ruling on Roe vs. Wade in 1973. What this accomplished was dropping the number of "unwanted" children.

There has been a fair bit of research on how "unwantedness" affects children and young adults as they develop. Levitt and Donohue explored a number of these in their initial paper that was published in 2001.[3] From the time infants are born until we reach adulthood (and honestly for our entire lives) the notion of being unwanted has a profound impact on people. Even an individual experience of being unwanted can be incredibly painful and leave a lasting impact for decades, and maybe our entire life. By eliminating a significant number of these unwanted births, this change in policy had ultimately led to a reduction in the number of people most likely to commit crimes.

As I write I recognize that there is a danger in including a study like this in our discussion because of its political and religious ramifications. Most of the Christian world is against abortion, and it would be easy to either dismiss this as liberal propaganda, or for a smaller number, celebrate this as an argument for freedom of choice. However, both of these reactions miss what this study says about us as humans. We are born with an innate need to be loved and valued. Growing up believing that we are unwanted is damaging. Even if we aren't driven to a life of crime, it profoundly impacts our sense of who we are and our worth.

Identity

In the previous chapter I referenced the idea that adolescence is essentially centered around the answering of three questions.

1. Who am I? (Question of **Identity**)

2. Where do I fit? (Question of **Belonging**)

3. What difference do I make? (Question of **Autonomy)**

In my mind, the first question, "Who am I?" really is foundational to the other two. I will have a hard time knowing where I belong and whether or not I matter if I don't first know who I am. Understanding our identity is essential to knowing what drives us, what we are afraid of, and why we make the decisions that we do. It dictates how we treat others and how we assign them value. The way we answer the identity question has a profound impact on virtually all of the decisions we make.

Before we get too far into the identity question, humor me by doing the following exercise. Take a few minutes and answer the question, "Who are you?" with reference to three different people: a) a complete stranger, b) an acquaintance at work, c) your spouse or best friend. If it is helpful, grab a notepad or your smartphone to write down the main points as they come to you.

What were your answers? Was this a difficult question to answer? Did you find that they were different based on who you were answering them for, or did they stay consistent? Was there anything that surprised you as you thought about it? Was it easier to describe yourself to a stranger, an acquaintance, or a close friend?

For some of us, describing who we are to a stranger or an acquaintance may be easier than someone we have a more intimate relationship with. We choose to talk about ourselves in regard to things like our job, people whom we are connected with, recreational activities, etc. We can pick and choose what people see and know about us to manipulate who they think we are. However, when having the conversation with someone to whom we are more intimately connected, it can be a bit tougher. If my wife or a good friend asks me this question, they aren't interested in me telling them about my job, my hobbies, or other socially identifying markers. The question begins to shift from "What do I want these people to think about me?" to "Who am I really, and what am I really willing to let other people know?" This question is intertwined with our sense of autonomy and belonging as well. For many people, this is challenging to define and they are unaware of how it is driving their decision-making.

I can illustrate this from my own experience. Growing up, I was quite shy and sensitive. I remember it taking all I had to keep from bursting into tears when my 5th grade teacher called me out for some minor trifle. I think I was generally well liked by the other kids, but I always felt as though I had to earn their approval. As I moved into middle school and high school, I began to develop strategies for showing people that I was valuable. I was a pretty good athlete and that led to a lot of connections with people. I didn't have to think of something to say to them if I could impress them with my athletics. Later I learned that I was fairly quick-witted and could take control of situations with humor and sarcasm. These were effective ways for me to gain the approval of others while minimizing any vulnerability. Through music, intellect, appearance, etc. I found ways to earn the approval of others, thereby feeling more valuable.

There are many different "identities" that people use to help them feel more valuable. Here are some of the ways that I've observed people define themselves.

- Occupation

- Athletics

- Physical Appearance

- Humor

- Organization (or the ability to organize)

- Control

- Popularity

- Efficiency

- Problem Solving

- Parenting

- Intellect

- Wisdom

- Productivity

Perhaps you have used some of these. Maybe you have a different list. When we get to the core of these items, each one is based on what we think makes us valuable. If I get my value from work, it is likely related to my ability to perform a task or create a product that others need, thereby demonstrating my importance to society. If my value comes from my physical appearance, then I am creating feelings of admiration and approval from the people around me. Maybe I feel valuable when I am in control, or when I am able to offer wisdom to the group. All of us will choose a different item on the list (or perhaps on another list), but the underlying need for each of us is the same. All of us have an innate need to feel valuable.

Here is the problem, everything on this list (and most anything else we might add) will eventually let us down. Eventually we can't run as fast, jump as high, throw as hard as we used to be able to. Eventually our beauty fades and we don't look so good. Eventually our intellect slows, and we struggle to exhibit the wit that we used to. (Evidenced by the existence of "dad jokes".) We will run into things we can't fix, problems we can't solve, situations we can't manage, relationships that can't be repaired, etc. When we do, we experience an assault on our sense of value. If the challenge is minor, we can generally survive. However, if the event is major, we will end up with serious questions regarding our identity and self-worth. This is the stuff of midlife crisis, bouts of depression, struggles with anxiety, etc., and it can be life-altering.

If you want to take things a step further, spend some time with the Enneagram Personality Test. Each different personality type is motivated by something different, but if we get to the core of each type, we will find what we feel makes us truly valuable. When I took the test a few years ago, I was a 98% type 3 (The Achiever), followed closely by type 7 (The Enthusiast) and type 9 (The Peacemaker). From what I shared earlier in this chapter, you might be able to see how I learned during my adolescent journey to make myself valuable to others through things I could do. I was looking for affirmation of my achievements. I can also tell you that being the "life of the party" and maintaining relationships were significant contributors to my feelings of self-worth, which is consistent with the other two personality types.

If you are looking to understand yourself or others better, exploring the Enneagram or a similar test is a great exercise in learning more about what motivates you, how you process the world around you, and how you manage your emotions. The great thing about this personality assessment tool is that it actually gives information about how each personality type tends to react when our sense of identity becomes threatened. It helps us understand our strengths and weaknesses in different circumstances. It can help us understand why the people around us act the way they do as well.

When we look at the process of adolescence, one of the primary tasks is for us to establish where our value comes from. However, if the church is full of people struggling to understand their own identity, there is no way anyone can adequately help others understand theirs. We become so busy trying to prove our value to others that showing them why they are valuable is the last thing on our mind. It causes us to be afraid to talk to the new person that walks into our church because we are worried about what they will think of us, or what we will say. It causes us to protect what is "ours" (worship style, color of the carpet, etc.) at all costs. We tend to look for opportunities during conversations with others to share the stories, knowledge, etc., that make us important instead of being interested in hearing theirs. At the least this creates unfriendly and unwelcoming church environments, at the worst it leads to toxic situations with the ability to inflict incredible damage and scarring on others.

Youth and young adult ministry is affected by this search for our own value in several ways. Finding volunteers to work with these ministries is difficult because most people are afraid. They are worried about how they will show these adolescents that they are cool enough to be listened to. On the flip side, those who do volunteer may do so as a part of their quest to stay awesome. (Note: in general younger people don't use the word "awesome". If you are trying to stay "awesome", you may have already failed.) When we walk into a group of teens or young adults we can easily be taken back to our high school/college days and begin to dig out some of our old coping mechanisms. We may gravitate toward the people who we would have felt more comfortable with when we were their age. Instead of listening to their stories we tell our own. Maybe we try to exert our control on the program. "We did this when I was a teenager, and it was awesome!" Or we may just decide that they don't want to hang out with us anyway and we take a more hands-off role.

Within the church we have essentially created a culture of unwantedness. While we may say nice things like, "I love it when the young people are involved" or "The youth are our future" or when we really want to look like we support youth and young adult ministries "They aren't our future, they are the church right now!", we haven't done the things that actually show them that they are valuable. Let's be honest, if the youth are our "future" or our "right now", why are they all leaving? Until we figure out a healthy understanding of where our own value comes from and learn how to show others that they are valuable, we will continue to scratch and claw to build and preserve our own sense of self-worth instead of helping them understand that they are valuable and wanted within our community. Through our actions, we will continue to demonstrate to teens and young adults that they aren't important, and we'll lose the privilege of being a part of their story.

Points to Ponder

1. Have you ever felt unwanted? What was the situation? How did you respond to it?

2. Who are you?

3. In what ways do you seek to make yourself valuable to others? Have any of these ever let you down?

4. What has your faith community done well to make teens and young adults feel wanted? Where could your faith community improve?

Understanding Our Own Identity

As I mentioned in the previous chapter, there are times in life when our identity and sense of self-worth are challenged. This happens multiple times each day on a small scale, but every so often something more major happens that significantly challenges our value. As I look back, I can think of a few such instances.

Relationships

One, or more accurately, three times during my adolescent journey I went through the experience of lost love. My first relationship was in seventh grade and lasted approximately a day and a half. I wrote her a note professing my love and even provided her with check boxes marked "yes" and "no" for her convenience. She checked "yes". The following day was filled with relational bliss. We spent the day skiing. We rode the chair lift together. She touched my hand. Life was beautiful. The following day I received a note that informed me that things wouldn't work out. Turns out I was a bit too short, among other things. (Rumor has it that there was actually a third party involved who brought us together, and then instigated our separation in order to become my sweetheart, but I digress.) The rejection was painful and reinforced the idea in the back of my mind that I wasn't good enough. I wasn't attractive enough. I wasn't cool enough. I wasn't valuable enough.

Thankfully over the next couple years I grew taller and in my junior and senior years of high school I took a couple more stabs at love. Through both of these experiences I did my best to morph into what I thought, or I was told I should be (see my Enneagram Profile in the previous chapter). But eventually, both ended in ways that affirmed that I wasn't good enough. While in hindsight I can see that these experiences were valuable and part of the journey that brought me to the amazing person I would ultimately marry, at the time they presented a direct assault to my sense of self-worth and created scars that took some time to heal.

Athletics

My sophomore year of college my friend James and I decided that we should be pro skiers. Modern freestyle skiing with half-pipes and terrain parks was just starting to take off, and we wanted to be a part of it. Over the previous couple years, we had spent countless hours watching VHS tapes of freestyle pioneers performing new tricks and practicing on the trampoline. We lived and breathed skiing. We began competing at various competitions around the Pacific Northwest and actually did pretty well, making some money and picking up some sponsors along the way. About halfway through the season we decided we were going to go all in. We scraped our funds together and signed up for the US Freeskiing Open in Aspen, CO. Training while going to school was tough, but I still found ways to do some cross training during the week and further practice on the snow every weekend. Then disaster struck. During an afternoon training session, I hit a jump at the wrong angle, missed the landing, and pancaked in the flats. Initially I was more concerned with what sounded like a large gong being pounded inside of my head as my helmet bounced off the snow. However, that was soon replaced by my inability to bear weight on my left knee. I had torn my ACL and Meniscus, and my season was done.

I was devastated. Skiing was who I was and what set me apart from other people. I didn't know if I would ever be able to ski at a high level again. That night I cried, not because of physical pain, but because of lost opportunity. I cried because I was disappointed. And I cried because I was an athlete, and I didn't know what I would be if that was no longer possible. Later I called my friend James to tell him the news.

"Guess what?" I said.

"You tore your ACL." He responded.

"Uh, yeah I did. But how did you know?"

"I tore mine a couple days ago, so it was a lucky guess."

A few weeks later we both underwent surgery one day apart, and spent the next week in a haze of pain relievers, movies, and video games. Having someone else journeying with me, who was a part of my story, helped encourage me and motivate me through my rehab. We never did become pro skiers, though skiing and the snowsports industry is a big part of both of our lives to this day. My identity as an athlete remained a significant part of who I was and a significant source of my sense of self-worth.

Ministry

I mentioned at the beginning of Chapter Two how circumstances had combined to make me feel like it was my job to be "Superpastor". Even though I began to see holes in that theory during my first few years in ministry, in many respects I continued to operate under that model. The apparent success of our youth program and the positive feedback from those around me continued to reinforce my behavior. That all changed in the beginning of my fourth year at my church when I made "The Mistake".

I won't go into the nature of my mistake here, but a poor decision on my part had resounding consequences within my ministry. It was an honest mistake but was also something that hurt people within my community that were very close to me. This happened about the same time that I was realizing how, despite being a part of a very successful ministry, I remained a deeply flawed human. Suddenly, I went from feeling like a rockstar to being filled with terror as to how my poor judgment would affect my ministry and the people around me. I felt like a fraud. I was the expert in youth ministry. I didn't make these kinds of mistakes. I had anxiety and insomnia for a month. When I did get up each morning, I would wonder if this was the day that people would finally find out that I was an imposter.

This experience left me deeply scarred. I felt trapped, like I had to find a way out of full-time ministry. While from the outside things were still going well and growing, I was planning my exit strategy. I began trying to get more volunteers involved and to offer more training. I spent more time investing in parents. (These were things I actually should have been doing more of all along.) My wife was graduating from her Physician Assistant program in about 6 months and our whole focus became about surviving until then before making our escape.

However, my escape plan went beyond a move to a different geographical location. I began looking at different career options as well, finally settling on physical therapy, given a prior interest in Orthopedics while I was in college. I felt suffocated by having my livelihood tied to my spirituality. It seemed like leaving was the only way to deal with the stress and guilt that I was feeling. When my wife graduated in June of 2008 we packed up, said goodbye to our friends, and ran.

This whole experience was a serious challenge to my sense of identity and value. My life had been based around youth ministry. I taught classes to other youth leaders on the subject. The teens in my program depended on me. I felt valuable, important to the wellbeing of the community. I was an expert. I knew things. Now I was starting a new career, from the beginning. While I was employed as a part-time pastor at Summit Northwest Ministries, I wasn't a "real pastor" in the eyes of those outside of my church. I would occasionally be asked by people about why I had "left the ministry." I still had my athletics (I was still involved in the ski industry) and other attributes that made me feel important, but I also found that I occasionally had to prove to others that I was valuable.

Thankfully, the church and community that I had moved into provided the ideal opportunity for my wife and me to heal and grow. When I was hired, the head pastor Ron told me, "I want you to do the things that make a difference in your life and help you grow spiritually and invite your friends. That's all I want."

This freedom combined with the love and grace I experienced within the community slowly began to heal my scars and help me grow to a greater understanding of my identity and where my value truly comes from.

Where Does a Healthy Identity Come From?

Here is what I learned. The only way to truly understand our identity and value is to learn from the One who created us. If my ultimate reality is rooted in my understanding of God, then my value as a living being must be based on this understanding. Instead of assessing my value based on what others, or even I think about me, I must default to the way that God thinks about me.

I've always known about grace. I've preached numerous sermons, taught small group sessions, and participated in many personal conversations where I have explained the idea of grace to others. I have dispensed grace to many people and seen it change their lives. But it was through the years of recovery from my first foray into pastoral ministry that I realized just how difficult it was to have grace for myself. While I know my friendship with God was only possible due to the grace that I was offered, there was still a part of me that felt as though I had to earn it.

During a Christian History class that was part of my theology degree at Walla Walla University (then Walla Walla College), I remember a conversation I had with my professor when we were discussing the difference between Martin Luther and Desiderius Erasmus. In case you don't have a degree in Christian Church history, Erasmus and Luther were two prominent theologians during the birth of the Protestant Reformation. At that time the Church was struggling with corruption and political influences that threatened to derail its mission of spreading the gospel. People could essentially buy their salvation with money or donations to the church. Those who spoke out against the Church were threatened with damnation and persecuted under the Church's political influence. Both Luther and Erasmus recognized the need for the church at that time to make changes.

Both of these theologians recognized the need for a return to an understanding of the human connection with God being dependent on grace. However, it was the role of the human component that led to a debate between the two. Luther believed that salvation and a relationship with God was solely dependent on grace. There was nothing that we as humans could do to earn it, or to un-earn it. He even struggled with the idea of humans "choosing" to accept grace, and instead argued that it was only through God's grace that they were able to make this decision. Erasmus argued that, while grace was necessary to provide the opportunity, humans also had a part to play in this process. While God offered grace to humans, it was their job to essentially meet in the middle. I remember having a good-natured debate with my professor Monte Buell as I tried to process this notion. I struggled to wrap my mind around the idea that the good things that I did, as well as the less desirable ones, didn't earn me something. It was several years down the road, and some difficult life experiences, before I began to truly understand the implications of grace.

Grace is Free

The funny thing about trying to earn grace is that if we could, it would no longer be grace. Merriam-Webster defines grace as "unmerited divine assistance given to humans for their regeneration or sanctification"[1] The unmerited nature of grace means that by definition it cannot be earned, bought, or stolen. This is confirmed by numerous Biblical examples.

"For God so loved the world that he gave his one and only Son, that whoever believes in him shall not perish but have eternal life." John 3:16 NIV

"But God demonstrates his own love for us in this: While we were still sinners, Christ died for us." Romans 5:8 NIV

These are just a few verses that illustrate God's love for us. God was willing to endure great sacrifice for the chance to be our friend. God was willing to do this while we were still sinners, enemies of the Kingdom.

Perhaps one of the best examples of this is a story Jesus told, known to most people as the Parable of the Prodigal Son. In this story there is a boy who grows tired of living at home. He comes to his father and asks for his portion of the inheritance early, essentially telling his father that he wished he was dead so he could have his money. His father doesn't argue but gives him his portion and lets him go his way. The son travels to a distant land where he ends up squandering his entire fortune on wild living. (Prodigal means "wastefully extravagant.") Eventually he finds himself penniless, homeless, and destitute. At one point Luke says that he longed to fill his stomach with the food that was given to the pigs he was feeding, but no one would give him anything.

At this point the story says that he came to his senses, realizing that the servants in his father's house were treated much better than he was. He decides to return and beg to be allowed to live as one of his father's slaves. But his father will have none of it.

"20 So he got up and went to his father. "But while he was still a long way off, his father saw him and was filled with compassion for him; he ran to his son, threw his arms around him and kissed him. 21 "The son said to him, 'Father, I have sinned against heaven and against you. I am no longer worthy to be called your son.' 22 "But the father said to his servants, 'Quick! Bring the best robe and put it on him. Put a ring on his finger and sandals on his feet. 23 Bring the fattened calf and kill it. Let's have a feast and celebrate. 24 For this son of mine was dead and is alive again;

he was lost and now is found.' So they began to celebrate." Luke 15:20-24 NIV

There are a couple of key ideas that are worth noting here. The first is that the son has done nothing to deserve his father's favor. He has come home as a last resort. Death was his only other option, and he had exhausted all others before he decided to return. He deserved to be rejected, berated, and cast out on the street.

But that is not what happened. Verse 20 says that his father saw him while he was a long way off, was filled with compassion for him, ran to him, threw his arms around him, and kissed him. This is before he even has a chance to launch into his pitch about why his father should allow him to come back as a servant. Instead of his father feeling angry, or indifferent, he was watching the road, hoping to see a familiar form making his return. When he did see his son returning, there was no thought of making him pay for what he had done. No steps were taken to ensure that the son met him halfway. No concern regarding what others might say. Overcome with the joy of his son's return and not wanting to spend another moment apart, he ran to him. When the son does try to argue his case, to do his part, his father will have none of it. Instead, he throws a party.

In his book *What's So Amazing About Grace?* Phillip Yancey describes an anecdote involving C.S. Lewis: "During a British conference on comparative religions, experts from around the world debated what, if any, belief was unique to the Christian faith. They began eliminating possibilities. Incarnation? Other religions had different versions of gods appearing in human form. Resurrection? Again, other religions had accounts of return from death. The debate went on for some time until C.S. Lewis wandered into the room. 'What's the rumpus about?' he asked, and heard in reply that his colleagues were discussing Christianity's unique contribution among the world's religions. Lewis responded, 'Oh, that's easy. It's grace.'"[2]

While there are some who question whether or not this interaction actually took place, and others who question the validity of Lewis's claim, the fact that Christianity is built on the notion of grace is undeniable. (As is the fact that the term "rumpus" is used far too infrequently in our time.) As Christians we speak of grace, sing songs about it, name children after it, write books about it, and even use it interchangeably with prayer at mealtimes. (All these different uses of the term can become quite confusing, as is evidenced by Aunt Bethany in the 1989 classic National Lampoon's Christmas Vacation.) And yet when it comes to actually applying this concept into our daily life experience, many of us struggle.

In another quote from his book Phillip Yancey writes, "Grace means there is nothing we can do to make God love us more—no amount of spiritual calisthenics and renunciations, no amount of knowledge gained from seminaries and divinity schools, no amount of crusading on behalf of righteous causes.

And grace means there is nothing we can do to make God love us less—no amount of racism or pride or pornography or adultery or even murder. Grace means that God already loves us as much as an infinite God can possibly love."³

Here is where many of us Christians start to get uncomfortable. We like the idea of being able to ask for forgiveness for our sins. We're okay with the majority of our salvation being a gift from God, but we still feel like what we do has to be worth something. "Yes" we say, "I know I am saved by grace, but what is my part?" We struggle to believe that something can truly be free. For many years my concept of grace was that it was free, as long as I tried my hardest and was making progress. Things felt really good when both of those were happening. However, when I made mistakes and struggled with sin in my life, I felt as though there was no way I would ever be good enough to be saved. I didn't doubt God's power, but instead my ability to respond in the way I needed to. I was struggling with holding up my end of the bargain.

Over the past decade of my own spiritual journey I've become more and more convinced that the desire to hold up our end of the bargain ends up robbing the gospel of its power. We end up living a version of Christianity that looks the part but doesn't have the ability to truly change who we are. We ask for divine assistance as WE wage war against sin in our lives, or at other times pretend that the ugly parts of us don't exist. We live what Bill Liversidge in his book and sermon series entitled

Victory in Jesus calls the "yo-yo" experience. His thoughts on this experience can be summed up as follows:[4]Things are going well. We're reading our Bible sometimes, praying a bit, listening to good sermons at church and generally treating people well. Then, we make a mistake. All of us have areas of darkness in our lives. Anger, pride, questionable integrity, substance abuse, pornography, greed, etc., it is different for everyone, but the results are the same. We feel shame and guilt along with a sense of being "out of relationship" with God. We spend a few hours, days, weeks in a funk with our shame and guilt. We beg for forgiveness and ask for more strength next time. Then, slowly the "good stuff" we do begins to catch up. We feel like we are making progress. Our good begins to outweigh the bad in our minds, and we feel spiritual again. We ride this wave until the next episode hits, and we repeat the process. As the cycle continues, we end up either riding an emotional rollercoaster, or becoming numb to the whole process as a way to cope.

The problem with this version of the Christian experience is that we end up focused on our performance. We alternate between pride regarding our progress, followed by shame and guilt when we fail. We do our best to let others see the "Christian" parts of us while living in fear that someone will discover the darkness that we can't quite seem to overcome. It's no wonder we as individuals and churches struggle to impact the community around us. We're so busy making sure no one finds out about the darkness in our own lives, while also trying to show others how good we are, that we don't have time to think about showing grace to others. And honestly, how could we if we have never really experienced grace ourselves?

"But wait a minute," you say, "Don't we all experience grace?" It depends on how you define the word experience. In a legalistic application of the term, we could say Jesus died for all, therefore all have experienced grace. However, to me the word has greater depth. In order to truly experience something, we must be affected by it. Oftentimes we as Christians like to describe grace like an algebraic formula.

Sinner + Jesus Death + Forgiveness - the penalty deserved = Grace.

While this is not incorrect information, It is possible for me to acknowledge the truth of the formula but not be affected by the application of it.

Let's say my family and I are visiting Yellowstone National park. On our way out the door of our hotel room my daughter grabs a book she has just begun reading to help pass the time. We reach the park entrance right as she begins chapter 3, drive by Old Faithful as she hits chapter 7, wait for a herd of bison to cross the road at chapter 9, swing by Grand Prismatic Spring halfway through chapter 12 (She stays in the car because she is in the middle of a really good part.) and finally arrive back at our room just as she finishes off chapter 15. Did she experience Yellowstone National Park? In the legalistic sense, yes. The park exists, she was in it, therefore she experienced it. Did her presence in the park affect her? Not really. She missed out on seeing the brilliant colors in the Grand Prismatic Spring, the sound and spray of old faithful, the two bison calves that were romping in the grass next to the road, the gurgling and blurping of the mud pots. She was physically present in Yellowstone, but did not experience it.

I am convinced that the primary reason most churches are struggling to make an impact on their local community is that they are filled with members who have never truly experienced the love and grace that God offers. When people do it changes them. Paul talks about this in 2 Corinthians 5. He writes that when we truly understand the grace that we have been given we are "compelled" to action, and we see people differently. We become a "new creation". The world around us is seen and interpreted through the lens of Jesus's love and sacrifice for us. Religion becomes more than just a list of things that we do and don't do to feel spiritual and earn favor with God. We love others and look for ways to serve, not to earn anything, but because that is just what people do who have experienced the love and grace of God in their lives.

Instead, we Christians tend to subscribe to what I call a "List Theology." We feel religious success is based on obtaining the correct list and adhering to it. Biblical study is based around making sure we have the right list. The better we keep our list, the more spiritual we feel. Evangelism becomes about proving that our list is the best. Salvation is based on one's ability to obtain and follow the right list. Unfortunately, while a list can modify behavior, it doesn't change hearts. There is no power in a list of rules, of things that one does or does not do to adhere to the code. And because none of us are able to keep it perfectly, we either give up or struggle with shame and guilt as we move in and out of "God's favor." Honestly, this isn't good news, which is why none of us want to go out and share it with others.

While I was a youth pastor in California, I took a group of my high school and college members to a Jeremy Camp concert. We arrived at the venue just as the concert was about to start, and we were hustling to try to get in for the first song when something caught my eye. By each of the entrances there were people stationed with signs that listed various things that "God Hates." Gays, Jews, Billy Graham, Psychologists, anyone who celebrates Christmas, the list went on. The people holding the signs berated those who passed by, giving them all the reasons that they were going to be damned to hell.

Like any self-respecting pastor, I had to go and learn more. I tried to engage a guy holding one of the signs in conversation and spent the next 15 min trying to get a word in as he spewed hate and hellfire on me and those who were passing by. He became really excited when he learned which religious community I am a part of and told me that my church founders were the "spawn of Satan." He didn't provide evidence for his assertions but made up for it with confidence and aggressive delivery. Apparently, the only way to avoid being burned and tortured forever was to join the one true church, conveniently named A True Church. For him, sharing the gospel (The Good News) was letting the world know that God was really mad, and their only chance at avoiding hell was to adopt his list. He didn't have any converts, and we missed the first half of the concert, for which my wife has still never completely offered me grace.

But what if God isn't mad at us? What if God loved us so much, He was willing to do whatever it took to have a friendship with us? What if God continued to feel this way about us, despite our many failures? What if we are valuable to God, not because of what we produce or as a result of keeping the right list, but because we are His creation? What if we never had to go through life alone? What if instead of having to earn our value, we were valuable because God thinks we are valuable? Wouldn't that be good news? Wouldn't we want to share that with the people around us?

I recognize that not everyone will come to the same understanding of grace that I have, and I'm sure mine will continue to evolve over time. Here is why I think this discussion is important. A true understanding of the Gospel tells us that our value is not based on what other people think about us, or even what we think about ourselves, but on what God thinks about us. Our true identity is as sons and daughters of God. (John 1:12, 1 John 3:1-2) God has adopted us into His family in order to share in "His Inheritance." (Romans 8:14-17) We didn't earn this. We simply allowed ourselves to experience and embrace the love and grace we have been offered. However, as children of God our value is infinite. The God of the universe thinks that we are amazing. The God of the universe was willing to become one of us and die to show us how valuable we are. This is our ultimate identity.

For me, understanding this has changed everything. I no longer have to prove my worth to others. I am no longer a slave to their opinions and approval. I have an answer to the voices in my head that tell me I'm not good enough. I still like to produce. I still am motivated to maintain relationships with others, and it feels good when others approve of me and what I do. But my identity no longer lives in this space. I am a child of God, and nothing on earth can change this ultimate reality.

The interesting part is that what I do doesn't look all that different from when my faith tended to be more list based. I still read my Bible, play worship music in church, do my best to serve others, try to be patient and kind to my family, etc. However, the reason I do it has changed. Instead of trying to earn–or in some cases avoid un-earning–something from God, I do these things simply as a response to the love and grace that I've experienced. I am disappointed when I fail to live up to where I want to be, but I also recognize that it doesn't change the way God feels about me. I am and will continue to be part of God's family. I have freedom to make mistakes. What a relief!

Release

A few months ago, I went on a quick backcountry ski tour behind my house. We had just experienced a storm that dropped six to eight inches of snow. When the storm began, it was cold and the first inch or two was light and fluffy. However, the temperature had climbed throughout the night until it was hovering right around freezing. The snow was beautiful, but it was also wet and heavy. As I traveled there were numerous trees and bushes that hung down over the trail I was on. Many appeared as though they were reaching their breaking point. They strained under the load of snow, and many looked as though they would never be the same.

As I approached one of these trees, I took my ski pole and tapped the low hanging branches. Because the storm was cold when it initially started snowing and then warmed up, the snow underneath was poorly bonded to the branches. In an instant all of the snow broke free. The branches, suddenly free of the crippling weight, whipped back into their normal position so quickly that I actually received a small wound on my cheek for my trouble. What before had been near the breaking point, now stood tall and full of new life. I spent the rest of my morning liberating trees as I traveled. The cut I received on my face in the first tree encounter did nothing to dissuade me. Some trees responded in a similar manner to the first. For others the process was slower and not as complete. It was going to take time for them to heal. However, they all experienced a transformation.

This is what experiencing grace feels like. This is the Gospel. If you have never experienced this before, spend some time with the parable of the Prodigal Son. Read about how Jesus treated people like the woman who was caught in the midst of an affair. (Tradition tells us this wasn't her first offense.) Read in Romans seven and eight about how Paul struggles but is not condemned. Create some time and space to let God help you understand the way He really feels about you. Ask to fully experience God's love and grace in your life. And once you do experience it? Well, then comes the fun part. You get to go knock the snow from some other trees.

Points to Ponder

1. Was there anything in this chapter that helped you to see the Gospel in a new light? If so, what was it?

2. Do you struggle to accept grace as a free gift? If so, why do you think it is challenging?

3. How has your faith community spread grace to those both within and outside? Where do you see the need for improvement?

4. Are there ways that a desire to "earn your value" influ-

ences your decisions? If so, what are they?

5. How do we balance the importance of seeking and proclaiming truth, with a Gospel based on grace? Where do you see this struggle play out in your own experience?

6. How have you experienced grace in your life?

UNDERSTANDING THE
IDENTITY OF OTHERS

Ownership imparts value. For a while my wife and I went through a phase where we would regularly watch a show called *Antiques Roadshow* on PBS. The creators of the show travel to various locations around the United States with a team of experts from auction houses and independent dealers to help locals assess the value of their antiques and collectibles. *Antiques Roadshow* cameras tell the story of family heirlooms, flea market finds, and items saved from attics and basements, while experts reveal the fascinating truths about these items. It wasn't flashy, there were no celebrity personalities or relational drama. Just real people hoping that great grandma's keepsake they discovered in the attic had more value than what met the eye.

Half the fun of the show was watching the humanity in their reaction, especially when items were found to have much more value than they had ascribed to them. This often happened with items that didn't have any inherent value, in and of themselves. In ordinary circumstances they would just be another piece of junk cluttering someone's garage. Instead, these pieces were valuable because of the identity of their owner or creator. A pocket watch that was passed on from a man's grandfather ultimately ended up being worth $3 million because it was made by Patek Philippe. A woman brought an oil painting of her grandmother that ended up being worth $500-$700K because it was painted by an American artist Robert Henri.[1] What at first appears ordinary and mundane has the ability to become incredibly valuable based on whose it is. This also is true when it comes to people.

The Value of Others

Suppose you and I are friends, and I happen to be in the neighborhood and drop by for a visit. You, being the close friend and excellent host you are, invite me in for a chat and perhaps a hot beverage. (English Breakfast Tea with cream and sugar for me...I'm fancy like that.) As we sit in the living room we connect over memories and future plans. We tell stories and laugh. Our hearts are filled with the warmth that is brought by connecting with an old friend. As our conversation continues, your little puppy (insert name here), or kitten if you are a cat person, wanders over and hops up on the couch next to me. This adorable little fur ball begins to nuzzle my arm and show its affection (purring, wagging tail, etc.). The cuteness is unbearable.

Now, imagine that as we continue to talk about the good old days, I take this heart-melting, loving, your-pride-and-joy furball and chuck it across the room. Maybe I stand up and drop kick it into the kitchen. Or maybe I'm more subtle and start pulling its tail, poking its eyes, and flicking its ears. Regardless of which form of unkindness I choose, what would your response be? What would happen to our friendship?

I have used this illustration with a stuffed animal model during a number of speaking engagements, and the response is always the same. Shock, horror, pure hate. One girl wouldn't speak to me the rest of the day because of how I had treated her pretend pet. Why the strong response? I didn't do anything to her. The answer goes back to value. You love your little Fifi or Fido (Fred in my son's cat's case), and my actions show a lack of trust and respect in our relationship, let alone an absence of good old human decency. We can't be friends if I am unwilling to value the things you value.

As we come to understand the way that God feels about us, it changes the way we see other people. 2 Corinthians 5 has been helpful in providing some Biblical basis for what we as humans intuitively know happens in everyday life. When I know that it drives my wife nuts if I place my damp towel on the bed after a shower, leave my laundry all over the bedroom, make loud noises, or in any way even pretend to have any intent of sticking my finger in her armpit, I'll do my best to avoid doing these things. It isn't because I want to earn something from her or to create leverage in some other situation. That's just what people who love each other do. I will love, value, and respect the things that she loves, values, and respects because that is how relationships work. I am willing to make some sacrifices because I know that happiness for both of us will be maximized as the relationship thrives.

When God calls or "commands" us to love one another, He is simply helping us understand that this basic human relationship principle also applies to our connection with Him. In fact, this love for our fellow humans is established in John 13 and 15 as an identifying marker of those who are Christ followers. By recognizing our true identity as a child of God, we also recognize the true identity of others. Ownership, or in this case, which family we are a part of, matters. And it isn't just Christians that God feels this way about. It is all humanity. His desire is that none will perish. That doesn't mean that none will; we've been given the ability to make our own choices and choose whether we want to reciprocate God's offer of friendship. But God loves and values every person, even if they choose not to return that love.

Evangelism's Dark Side

Many Christians don't like the word *evangelism*. For some it brings up painful past experiences, while others feel that the whole process is manipulative. A couple of years ago I had a conversation that illustrates the dark side of evangelism that causes some of us to recoil at the suggestion. Lana (not her real name) was a sweet and kind woman in her early 70's who came to see me at my physical therapy office, following a knee surgery. In her first appointment she let me know in a non-offensive way that she was a Christian and that she would love to talk to me about Jesus if I was interested. When she learned that I was also a pastor she was excited to engage further.

Over the next couple weeks, we had some great discussions in which we were able to process theological ideas. Lana came from a Baptist background, which has some similarities, as well as some differences when compared to my own religious community. We had a great time discussing some of these differences and processing them together. She knew her Bible cover-to-cover and loved to talk about it. After a couple weeks she mentioned how much she enjoyed our conversations, and then shared a story that had caused her to be a bit skeptical when we first met.

Lana lived alone on a fixed income and quite frankly, struggled financially. Furthermore, her knee issues made walking difficult, and she struggled to keep up with things around the house. A few years prior, a group of people from a local church from my own religious community came and knocked on her door. Somehow, they had learned that she needed help and had brought her some food. Over the next few weeks, they came another time or two to bring food and provided some help around the house. On maybe their third visit they invited her to some meetings that were being held at their local church. Lana kindly told them that she had a deep relationship with Jesus and that she probably would not be attending but thanked them for the invitation. She could tell that they were disappointed as they left, and she never saw or heard from them again. Apparently, their interest in helping her was motivated only by their desire to share their theological "list." Once they realized that she wasn't going to be their next convert, they moved on, leaving her feeling lonely and abandoned.

Stories like Lana's make my heart hurt. Unfortunately, her's is not an uncommon one. When our desire to reach out to others is driven by a need to convince others that our "list" is better than theirs, our true motives quickly become evident. We care more about proving our rightness than sharing love and grace. The good news becomes less about God's love and more about legalism. Success is measured by how many people are willing to adopt our list as their own, and often the end justifies the means. Fear, guilt, and other forms of emotional manipulation are frequently employed to help spread the "good news." This type of "evangelism" not only has limited success but frequently does more harm than good. Even those who do respond often struggle in their new community. While a list can modify behavior, it rarely leads to a heart change.

However, if we look in the gospels, we see a very different picture. The Greek word for evangelism *euangelizo* literally means "to bring good news." Jesus said in Luke 4:18-19 (NIV), "The Spirit of the Lord is on me, because He has anointed me to proclaim good news to the poor. He has sent me to proclaim freedom for the prisoners and recovery of sight for the blind, to set the oppressed free, to proclaim the year of the Lord's favor."

Jesus's ministry revolved around showing people that they were valuable, especially those whom society had cast aside. Frequently those around him–including his disciples–were shocked at the people he would interact with. The poor, sick, blind, prostitutes, tax collectors, women in general, all were seen as second class (or worse) by the society he lived in. Religious leaders of the day would intentionally avoid many of these people and taught that their trials in life were a punishment from God. But not Jesus. He saw people differently. He specifically sought the outcasts, the downtrodden, those filled with guilt and shame. When He found them, He didn't present them with a list of things they should do or not do in order to be holy. He didn't invite them to the sermon on the mount or some temple meetings. Instead, He offered them love and grace in the midst of their situation. He healed them, fed them, and touched them. Instead of telling them how awesome He was so they would follow him, He let them know that the God of the universe loved them.

That's good news. The God who created the universe loves humans who have done nothing worthy of earning His favor, and in many cases have actually worked against His kingdom, enough to become one of us and die to prove His love. This concept is insane if we really think about it. Romans 5:6-8 (NIV) puts it this way, "You see, at just the right time, when we were still powerless, Christ died for the ungodly. Very rarely will anyone die for a righteous person, though for a good person someone might possibly dare to die. But God demonstrates his own love for us in this: While we were still sinners, Christ died for us."

That is the Gospel. In a world that tells us we aren't good enough, smart enough, attractive enough, productive enough, religious enough, etc. God tells us we have incredible value. He wants to adopt us into His family. A response to this knowledge is what gives the Gospel its power. When we respond to God's love and grace, and leave behind the shame and guilt that holds us, it changes us. We experience freedom. We become the "new creation" that 2 Corinthians 5 talks about, and we begin to see the world differently. We experience true, honest-to-goodness joy.

I believe the challenge with evangelism for many of us is that we have never really allowed ourselves to experience God's love and grace in our own lives. We are good at saying the right words but struggle to believe that they are true. We desperately cling to our list of things that we do and don't do, trying to be good enough to feel like we deserve this grace. We struggle to share the good news of how God feels about us because we haven't truly been able to experience it. Sharing our faith becomes about showing other people we are awesome or cool enough so that they will want to adopt our list. That doesn't sound like much fun to most of us, unless you like to argue and debate, in which case you may feel a rush of adrenaline and smug superiority as you annihilate the lists of others with your systematic theology.

Let's discuss "the list" for a moment. I have written a lot about our list of beliefs and the problems that it can cause. However, this isn't the fault of the list. Doctrine is incredibly important. I belong to my religious community because the particular list of doctrines makes the most sense as I read and study scripture. Every single doctrine I embrace helps me understand more about who God is, what God values, and how incredible the love and grace offered to me are. The list is good. But it doesn't earn me anything. God doesn't like me better because I have a better list. My list just helps me understand and respond to His love.

Picture this. You and I have a mutual friend named Ben. (This is not a reference to any of my actual friends named Ben, as there are several, and all are stand-up guys.) Let's say we both really like hanging out with Ben. He is good natured, tells better-than-average jokes, is game for most anything, frequently helps out his friends if they are in need, and quite honestly is a bit of a people magnet. Ben also has that ability to make everyone feel important, and he sure appears to genuinely care about people. However, I have been told by a third party that in his spare time Ben enjoys torturing puppies. (Yep, here we go again with the baby animal thing.) This changes how I respond to Ben. Even though he seems like a pretty cool guy, this information changes the way I think about him.

Now, let's say you know this information is untrue. You know that Ben actually loves puppies, volunteers weekly at the local animal shelter, and is an activist for puppy rights. Wouldn't you want to share this information with me? Of course. And in doing so, you just shared an important "doctrine" about Ben. The value in this "doctrine" is not that I can now prove to Ben that I know he loves puppies, therefore earning me special favor. Instead, the "doctrine" you shared with me helps deepen my friendship with Ben, and also prevents me from turning him in for animal cruelty. Our list serves a valuable purpose because it helps us understand who God is and how much we are loved. However, just because we may have a more-or less-accurate list doesn't mean we are better or worse friends of God than the people around us. It just helps us in building that friendship.

So, our job as Christians is really just to fully experience the love and grace that God offers us in our own lives. The natural response of having our lives made better by this process is that we will want other people to experience it, too. At its core, evangelism is simply helping others understand how valuable they are. If we aren't wanting to share this with others, we probably need to create some time and space for us to experience the Gospel ourselves. We will begin to see others through the lens of the gospel, to recognize the value that each of them has as sons and daughters of God.

Shut Down

I recently stopped by the high school youth room at our church to connect with our youth pastor and the teens who were attending that week. (Alright, I'll be honest. I really just wanted some of their tater tots that I could smell from downstairs.) On my way out I passed one teen who was just arriving. He is the son of one of my friends and as I passed, I smiled and gave him a jaunty greeting. His response shocked me at first. With a sullen look on his face, he stared me down for a moment and then continued walking on by as if I wasn't worth his time.

There was a time in my ministry when I would have spent the next several hours trying to figure out what was wrong with me, or what I had done wrong. There were also times when my response would have been sarcastic, in an attempt to show that his response didn't hurt me. However, as my life has been changed by experiencing love and grace, I am now able to see past the assault on my own value and recognize that this adolescent is just trying to figure out where his own value comes from. He lives in a world that constantly tells him he isn't good enough, and he needs to be something he's not. It isn't about me. I am free to focus on looking for ways to show him that I value him, as opposed to trying to prove my own worth.

Points to Ponder

1. Why do you think that the Christian faith community struggles to see the value of certain groups of people? Who does your faith community struggle to offer love and grace to?

2. Can you think of any instances where you have seen or experienced evangelism's dark side? What happened? What were the effects?

3. What are some ways your faith community has been effective at spreading love and grace to the surrounding community? What are some ways that it can improve?

4. What are steps that you can take to better spread the Gospel to the people around you?

5. Why do you think many of us tend toward feeling like

we earn something with our theological list? How can
we avoid this?

INTERESTED VS. INTERESTING

There is a phenomenon that many describe within the Christian journey where our most profound spiritual experiences happen when we are most depleted. I've heard numerous stories of people who had to reach the "pit of despair" before they experienced a spiritual breakthrough. Some of our most effective ministry moments come about at times when we are most empty. Have you ever wondered why this is?

Scripture contains a number of examples of this as well. Elijah–who was an Old Testament rock star–had his life threatened, reached complete exhaustion, required supernatural intervention to even survive, and finally hid himself in a cave before he was able to hear God's voice. This was even after he experienced God bringing fire down from heaven. Another example is Peter, an expert fisherman, who failed his best friend and then later went a whole night of catching nothing before he responded to Jesus's call to spread the Gospel. These are just a few moments where we see people experience a low before they have a spiritual awakening or are called to a mission. Paul references this process in 2 Corinthians 12:9 (NIV) when he says, "But he said to me, 'My grace is sufficient for you, for my power is made perfect in weakness.' Therefore, I will boast all the more gladly about my weaknesses, so that Christ's power may rest on me."

I've heard Christians over time when discussing this phenomenon talk about life being too easy, and almost speak wistfully of encountering hard times in order that they or the people around them will be more spiritual. While I don't think we are called to seek out pain and suffering to deepen our spiritual experience, I've also wondered what it is about us as human beings that creates this dynamic. Why do we have to reach the end of our rope before we experience growth? Why is God's power made perfect in our weakness?

I can't claim to understand all the nuances of this process. However, I wonder if the concept of understanding our true identity plays a significant part. Peter was one of the disciples. However, he was also prone to squabbling with the other eleven about who was the greatest and most important. His idea of ministry was to be awesome for Jesus. The night he denied his best friend, his identity as "Jesus's greatest follower" was shattered. The very thing he had boasted would never happen had come true. This was a direct assault on his self-worth. Even after he had seen Jesus resurrected, His response was to return to his boat and his nets. This was his identity prior to becoming Jesus's "dopest disciple." (If you don't know what this means, ask a teenager.) It is what he knew. He felt more in control. He was a fisherman. He could do this. However, after a night with no fish, he realized that he was bad at that, too. It was in this place that he was finally ready to accept the identity that Jesus wanted him to embrace. He was finally able to experience grace when Jesus offered it and began to see the world differently.

It wasn't as though Peter hadn't been involved prior to this experience. He had been with Jesus, he had done miracles, he had helped feed the 5,000, he was one of Jesus's closest three friends. However, it wasn't until he was able to see past his "Awesome for Jesus" identity that he was ready to truly change the world.

Best Date Ever

My wife and I have been together for 23 years, married for 19. (And let's be honest, the fact that she not only agreed to be my life partner but has continued to put up with my shenanigans for over two decades is one of the greatest exhibitions of grace you'll ever encounter.) However, I still remember what the experience was like back when I was a part of "the scene." Let's take a first date for example. You identify someone you regard as attractive and want to get to know better. Maybe you've met before but are now interested in establishing a more intimate relationship. Maybe you are adventurous and accept the offer of a blind date. Or perhaps, you and a friend agree to be back-up dates, since the guys who were initially going to a play at the community college with your potential date and her cousin might not be able to attend and quite frankly, you have nothing better to do. (Oddly specific I know...)

Preparation in such situations frequently begins days before the actual event. Maybe you pick out the clothes you plan to wear, think about the stories you may tell, do some research on your date so you know what they are into. Then again, maybe you are a back-up date and chances are, your services won't be needed anyway.

Finally, the day arrives, and you want to put your best foot forward. You fix your hair, you brush your teeth...you bathe. From there, you embark on an evening where two individuals do their best to prove their value to each other. Perhaps over dinner. Maybe while taking part in some shared recreational pursuit. Or maybe you and your friend are in the back seat of your date's dad's red 1970s Porsche 911 hanging on for dear life but trying to act casual.

The location doesn't matter, but the game tends to be the same. Two people desperately try to prove to each other that they are attractive, valuable and worth getting to know better. They recount stories, tell jokes, list their accomplishments, all in an effort to make the other person think they are interesting enough to establish a relationship with. While this process can be fun, it also tends to be stressful, and can be exhausting.

I had a conversation with a friend a while back who was beginning a foray back into the dating scene. For a number of years, he had mostly avoided making an effort to go on dates because of the stress and anxiety associated with it. When we talked, I was in the middle of processing my understanding of identity and decided to put my ideas to the test. I told him, "If you want to have the best date ever, focus on being *interested* not *interesting.*"

We talked a bit more about starting conversations and using the phrase, "Tell me more about that," to encourage his date to tell her story and then to affirm her in it. With that he went on his way, and I waited eagerly to hear how things went. When we had a chance to talk a couple days later, he reported that the two of them had a great time. Most of the awkwardness that he at times felt as an introvert was gone because he didn't feel the pressure to be funny, exciting, etc. He was able to focus on listening to his date's story and then engaging in it. He spent the evening affirming her value as opposed to trying to prove his. I felt like a proud (and of course very wise) parent.

I don't include this story because it shows any brilliance on my part. I am far from a relationship guru, as my wife could easily attest. These are basic relational concepts I learned in my college counseling class and youth pastor training I attended long ago. However, as my concept of identity has grown, I have given the same advice to a number of people who are nervous about going on dates, and the results are generally the same. People are longing to have their story heard, to be known by someone else and valued for who they are. All of us as humans are looking for a safe place to let our guard down. Whether or not the relationship continued on to something deeper, my friend had created a space where his date was able to tell her story and was valued. They had made a connection that they both could appreciate, whether or not it ultimately led to wedded bliss.

Not Just for Romance

One of the biggest barriers I hear from older generations when we talk about connecting with younger generations (or really anyone we don't know) is that they don't know what to say. They don't feel like the person is going to want to hear from them, and they believe they will be judged. Many live with this underlying sense of guilt, feeling that they should reach out to other people, but their fear of not knowing what to say or being judged harshly keeps them from acting on what they feel they should do.

Interestingly enough, I frequently hear a similar story from young adults when I talk to them about connecting with older generations. Recently one young adult told me, "Why would I talk to those people? All they are going to do is judge me." When I asked her why she thought that was, she responded, "They won't like the clothes I wear or the music I listen to. They will think that my job isn't good enough. All they are going to do is judge me." I didn't mention to her that the style of clothes that she was wearing was remarkably similar to the clothes the people she thought would judge her were wearing 20 years ago.

As I dug a little further, much of this sentiment wasn't based on any actual conversation with someone from an older generation. It was projected on them, the same way that older generations will project thoughts and feelings on younger ones about how they are perceived. What did strike me was that people of all ages are worried that if they make themselves vulnerable enough to connect with someone, that they won't be valued and instead will be judged and condemned.

Earlier I mentioned that while I was working as a youth pastor, I noticed an interesting pattern with the volunteers that I would bring on as a part of my team. For starters, it can be hard to get people who were actually willing to come and be a volunteer in the youth department. There were a lot of different excuses that were used, but ultimately most were just afraid that they wouldn't be effective or wouldn't know what to say. Those who did eventually agree to be a part of the ministry would often, at some level, revert back to the same behaviors they used in high school to try to create value for themselves. They would choose certain groups of kids to join with whom they felt comfortable. They would tell jokes or stories of epic exploits from "back when I was your age" as a way to try to prove that they were cool enough to talk to.

Others would huddle over in the corner and only engage with other adults. They were so worried about what the teenagers thought about them that they were unable to do much beyond bringing doughnuts and offering rides. I still appreciated the fact that they were willing to be involved. However, their focus on their own value impaired their ability to create meaningful connections with the teenagers they were attempting to serve.

Here's what they, and I for many years, didn't completely understand: the truth is, almost all of us, young or old, are looking for the same thing. We are looking for people who will value us for who we are. People who are a safe place. I didn't need youth leaders who were rock stars. Having shared areas of interest and being able to do some "cool stuff" can be a conversation starter. But what I really needed was people who understood where their value came from. I needed people who didn't have to worry about proving themselves, and instead could look for ways to show the teens they were working with that they were valuable.

I needed people who were *Interested* not *Interesting*.

When we feel like we have to prove we are awesome so people will listen to us talk about Jesus, our ministry becomes about us. We have to choose the right stories, give our testimony in just the right way, maintain the right hairstyle and clothing. Maybe we swear just enough or tell borderline jokes to try to fit in. Or maybe we feel our job is to model the perfect Christian life. Never allow them to see any weakness on our part. Be a "good example". Either way, our ministry hinges on us proving how important we are in hopes that they will want to be like us.

The Alternative

When I used to hang out with John, he was probably in his mid 60s. It was during my youth pastor days in Fresno, California, and I would frequently drive out to Monterey and Santa Cruz to surf when my schedule afforded it. I was introduced to John by a friend on one of my trips, and we hit it off. Decades earlier he had started a surf fin company, and while he had mostly retired and passed the business on to his son and daughter, he still continued to hang out and play with different fin designs and materials. He surfed every morning and kitesurfed every afternoon when the wind kicked up. In addition to his prominence in the surf industry, he also ran a local youth ministry at a high school and always had a few teens he was mentoring.

John was my hero. He introduced me to kitesurfing, or as he called it, fly fishing for great whites. He gave me local knowledge on where to find the world's best strawberry shortcake (I'm not even joking). We connected over talking about both the thrill and frustration of youth ministry. John lived the life I wanted to live, and he gave me something to aspire to.

Here's the thing about John. I don't recall him ever once trying to educate me on how awesome he was. In fact, I learned about most of his exploits from mutual friends who passed on information that they had learned from some other source. (It was like hearing stories about the epic exploits of Chuck Norris.) He never once regaled me with stories of his surfing prowess, his contributions to the surfing industry, or even his successful youth ministry. That doesn't mean we didn't talk about those things from time to time. However, it was apparent that John didn't have anything he needed to prove to me. He loved God. He loved people. He spent his time focusing on those two groups.

While surfing was a vehicle that allowed him to connect with me in a unique way, he didn't need it to show me that he was cool enough to learn from. He listened to my story and validated me in it. (Though one time I did ask him why he hadn't sponsored me when I sent him my wakeboarding resume back in college.

He responded that if I didn't suck, he might have thought about it. Then he laughed.) He wasn't a perfect mentor and was just as much a flawed human as anyone else, but he let me know that I was valuable. While he had the traits and skills to be as "interesting" as they come, he chose to be "interested" and joined me in my journey.

Points to Ponder

1. Can you think of someone in your life who took the time to listen to your story? Who were they and what happened?

2. Can you think of ways where you find yourself attempting to be *Interesting* instead of *Interested*? What are some of them?

3. What are some of the barriers that keep you from talking to teens and young adults and learning their story? How about older generations?

4. How might your interactions be different if proving your own value was not a distraction?

MIND THE GAP

I grew up in a small town. For most of my life under the age of 25 I lived in Sandpoint, Idaho. Our population was somewhere around 10,000 people. At that time culturally it was a mix of 1/3 Hippie, 1/3 Yuppie, and 1/3 Redneck. We had a mall...sort of. There were a couple of grocery stores, including the now defunct Herald's IGA where you could go to the deli and order a kid's meal that included two deep fried burritos, two deep fried jojos, and a deep-fried cookie, all for a dollar. (It was the perfect post ski or wakeboard meal.) We spent most of our time doing the things small town kids do: riding bikes, jumping off bridges into the river, playing basketball at the park, etc.

Something we did not have in this small town setting was any semblance of a public transportation system. There were a couple of taxis in town, an Amtrack station, and that was it. If you wanted to go somewhere you begged a ride off your parents or rode your bike. Because of this it was always a bit of an adventure traveling somewhere on a plane or visiting a city where subways and buses are the norm. I still get just a little bit excited deep down inside when I get the chance to ride a train somewhere or hop on a plane.

One thing I learned about when I began venturing into cities, or traveling overseas, was "The Gap". For those of you with a rural background like me, the gap is the space between the door of a train or subway car, and the platform. I remember my first trip to Washington, D.C. when I was a freshman in high school. When we were on the subway platform there was typically a yellow line maybe 8" back from the drop off down to the tracks. This was an indicator of how close one could stand and avoid being hit by the subway train as it came through the station. (We knew this because we tested it, much to the ire of our adult sponsors.) Typically, behind that line was painted the words "Watch the Gap" or something to that effect. This served as a warning to avoid falling in the crack between the car and the platform when you entered or exited. As I have traveled to different places around the world, there is usually some sort of warning painted on the floor, on signs, or even announced over an audio speaker to encourage passengers to watch their step. My personal favorite is the British version "Mind the Gap."

The Generation Gap

The term "Gap" has also been used to describe a social divide as well. The term "generation gap" was coined in the 1960s by an editor at *Look* magazine named John Poppy. He used it to describe the divide in politics, tastes, morals, etc., between the Baby Boomers and older generations. Apparently, he adopted this term as a play on the Cold War term "missile gap." In the decades since, this term has been used to describe the differences of belief, politics, and values between older and younger generations.

I doubt I'm surprising many people when I say that the generation gap is widening. In 2018 the Pew Research Center published a report that indicated that the generation gap was as wide as ever when it came to a number of different political issues.[1] More recently issues such as gender identity, COVID, and others have further polarized younger and older generations. I don't think many of us need researchers to remind us that we live in a divided world. Furthermore, this widening has been accompanied by a decrease in cross-generational communication. We struggle to have conversations with people who think differently than us. Older generations have used terms such as "entitled", "snowflake", and "flaky" to describe younger generations. Younger people describe older generations as "judgmental", "close minded" and "intolerant". Even the words we use have different meanings to different generations, causing confusion when and if cross generational communication is attempted. Much of the time, conversations become more about "defending what is ours" than truly seeking to understand the viewpoint of the other person. This is especially true when looking at the topics of politics and religion.

When it comes to churches the generation gap is quite evident. There are many churches that are completely devoid of younger members. There are fewer churches that are composed primarily of younger members with no older generations present. Even in the few churches that have a strong representation of all ages, there is typically little cross-generational interaction.

I remember a baptism that I was part of a number of years ago that drove this point home. We had traveled to the coast with a small group of teens and parents for a baptism in the Pacific. We gathered on the beach around a fire while the adults in the group affirmed the decision of the young adult who had decided to take this momentous step. The water was cold, even with our neoprene baptismal robes (wetsuits), but it didn't matter. I had the opportunity to welcome this young man into a new life in Jesus, surrounded by some of his close friends as the surf crashed around and over us. It was a beautiful experience and one of the more unique baptisms I have been a part of.

However, I was intrigued by what happened afterward. Once the "official" portion of the experience was done two very distinct groups became evident. All the parents gathered around the fire and talked about adult stuff. All the kids moved over to a different part of the beach and had their own conversations. It was a little ironic that the people who had actually been in the cold water moved away from the fire while the people in coats stayed put.

Now, often when I bring up instances like this, people say things like, "Oh, those boys just want their space." Or "They need to be alone in their own groups." And they aren't necessarily wrong. However, I believe we frequently miss opportunities for connection and mentorship because other generations "need their space." In this particular scenario, I went over and joined the group of boys. They were excited to talk about the things that were happening in their life. They told me about their most recent recreational pursuits, things they hoped to accomplish,and funny stories about their friends. It wasn't awkward and their appreciation for someone instilling value in them was apparent.

I don't include this story to toot my own horn or convince you of how great a youth minister I am. I frequently am the one who stays at the fire, and likely if this was not a specific area of focus for me, I would have missed my opportunity.

It would also be a mistake to make the assumption that these adults were not investing in their kids. There was a significant push in this community to invest in their teens and young adults. They were serious about being involved in their sons' and daughters' lives, and made an intentional effort to spend quality time with them. However, even in a community that made a concerted effort at intentional parenthood, the gap between generations caused them to miss out on an opportunity.

Barriers to Communicating Across the Divide

When we do find opportunities to communicate, there are some other barriers that make having conversations more difficult.

Politics: Political ideology changes generation to generation.[2] Of course there are conservatives and liberals and the whole spectrum in between in every age group. However, each generation tends to take on its own particular flavor based on their shared experiences. This tends to put different generations in opposition to each other. It's amazing how political ideas have a way of shutting down communication. There are very few people who are interested in hearing and understanding the way that someone else processes the world politically. Most political conversations revolve around us protecting what we see as ours and trying to prove why others are wrong. They are not relational.

Religious Beliefs: These tend to be difficult because of the ramifications. If I am wrong about my religious beliefs, I might go to hell. Religion is also something that frequently is a part of our core identity. It is part of a foundation that when destabilized, causes us to become defensive and can evoke a fight or flight response. Dr. Alden Thompson, one of my theology professors who many know by his street name "AT" (Those who know, know.) would always tell us that the Bible is a casebook, not a codebook. This means we are not presented with a list of beliefs, but instead a list of stories from which we form our beliefs about God. We all have different life experiences and backgrounds, which cause us to interpret parts of scripture differently. This tends to be true generationally as well. As the gap widens between generations in this area, it tends to strain relationships.

Interests/Preferences: Different interests and preferences tend to limit our time of shared experience. Shared experiences draw people together. They give us common ground that makes relational connection easier. However, as generational preferences change, we just don't overlap as much. One generation may prefer one kind of church music to another, and they end up at different churches. One generation prefers to communicate by text while the other one may tend toward verbal communication. Older generations tend to become less active while younger generations may want to explore the world. Younger generations may choose gaming over other forms of recreation, which may leave older generations baffled. These differences not only limit shared experiences, but they also provide opportunities for judgment and condemnation.

Morals and Values: Along the same lines of religious beliefs, morals and values tend to be foundational pieces that help us process the world around us. Something as simple as a man holding a door open for a woman can cause friction. Issues of gender and sexuality, immigration and poverty, work ethic, etc., can all create barriers to connection and act as a wedge that further divides us.

These are just a few of the barriers that challenge us as we seek to reach across the divide. All too often, proving the superiority of our way of thinking becomes more important than being a bridge to the other side.

Should We Even Build Bridges?

At this point I need to note an interesting response that I have encountered as I have discussed the idea of connecting with other generations. Occasionally I will hear members of primarily older generations respond with, "Why does it matter?" or "This is just part of growing up." One gentleman I spoke to recently suggested that it was actually necessary for young adults to leave the church in order for them to discover their own identity and faith. He believed that it was healthy for them to disconnect from the community. Another simply felt that it wasn't important for them, or anyone to go to church. They could have faith on their own and we shouldn't really worry about whether or not they were a part of our community. There are members of older generations that believe there is little value in worrying about whether there are cross-generational connections.

I think I understand where some of these sentiments come from. Young adults do need to develop their own identity and faith. They need some space to do this. However, there is a difference between space within a mentoring relationship vs. space via abandonment. I think that sometimes these ideas are also fueled by a feeling of inadequacy in connecting with younger generations, or at times just our own selfishness.

In their book, *Growing Young* Kara Powell, Jake Mulder, and Brad Griffin outline the following benefits to church communities when younger generations are involved.[3]

More Service: Younger generations are motivated to serve, and tend to get the rest of the church community involved as well.

More Passion: Younger generations tend to have a lot of energy and pour themselves into whatever they do. This tends to help energize older generations as well.

More Innovation: Young people see life differently and will frequently bring new and innovative ways of approaching problems and opportunities if given a seat at the table.

More Money: Churches with an active young adult population tend to attract older members who support their ministries financially.

More Overall Health: Communities with all generations represented are more well rounded. A church that reaches 20-year-olds will also tend to reach 60-year-olds. However, a church designed to reach 60-year-olds will not reach 20-year-olds.

They also reported that there was an overall sense of more "vitality" in churches with a strong young adult population. These are the things that we miss out when we don't have young adults as a part of our faith community.

I would also like to circle back to our previous discussion of identity and value. The questions of identity, value, and belonging aren't just questions of adolescence. They are questions of humanity. At our core, our identity as children of God gives us a foundation to build on. However, our unique gifts and specific traits make us suited for a specific niche in the family of God. I believe that as members of older generations, we are functioning in our greatest capacity when we are able to take the wisdom gained from life experience and use it to mentor younger generations. Both parties benefit from this type of experience and the community grows stronger.

The Catch

But here's the catch. In order to experience these benefits, we have to recognize the value of younger generations and be willing to allow them a seat at the table. We need to value their place in our community, even if we don't always agree with them.

Templeton (He chose his character name, not me.) was a freshman in college when he showed up at my church and began hanging out with our teens and young adults. He was funny, the life of the party, and quickly became one of the leaders within the community. He had little experience with religion prior to joining our group, but jumped in wholeheartedly. He didn't have all the answers, but he wanted to follow Christ and help others experience the gospel as well.

Within a few years he let me know that he had decided to be a pastor, and I began to look for ways to get him experience in ministry. He started teaching in our middle school program and was soon asked to do a chapel service at a local Christian school that our church supported. He decided to talk about prayer and put hours into preparing. Finally, the day arrived, and I waited to hear about how it went. A few hours later he gave me a call, and by the end of our conversation I was furious.

Things were going smoothly until he reached the part of his presentation where he wanted to emphasize how much God wants to communicate with His children and build a friendship. "In fact," Templeton said, "You can just say, 'Hey God' and tell him about how your day is going." At this point, the vice principal Mr. Thag (If I'm going to make up names, they might as well be interesting. Feel free to insert your own quip about being stuck in the stone age here.) stood up and interrupted him mid-sentence. "Don't you think that is pretty disrespectful?" he said. He then let Templeton know in front of all the students that his ideas were inappropriate and he effectively ended the chapel.

I have to say, Templeton handled it well. (He still went on to become a pastor, so apparently he is a glutton for punishment.) As for our vice principal friend, when I went and talked to him about how he had responded to the situation, he made it clear how little regard he had for younger generations. The fact that he disagreed wasn't the issue. What really bothered me was that I was quite certain he would never have done that to me, and for sure would not have done it to the head pastor, even if we were preaching the same message. He wasn't interested in hearing the perspective from another generation, and showed through his response that he felt he didn't need to treat him with dignity or respect because he was young.

Incidents like these happen all too frequently in faith communities. I get angry just thinking about them, because I know the damage that is done to the receiving parties. However, my anger is accompanied by a deep sadness when I realize the missed opportunities that are associated with them. Mr. Thag missed out on the chance to connect with Templeton and have a deep, meaningful conversation about the nature of God. He missed the opportunity to provide ongoing mentorship and guidance. He missed the chance to be rejuvenated by Templeton's energy and enthusiasm. Templeton never had the opportunity to learn from Mr. Thag's years of experience. He missed the chance to have another stabilizing influence in his young adult journey. They both missed the opportunity to experience a cross-generational connection and the growth that comes with these relationships, and as a result, the next generation of kids missed a prime opportunity to experience the fullness of the Body of Christ.

Points to Ponder

1. Where do you see the greatest differences between older and younger generations? Have you seen anyone younger or older who was effective at bridging this gap? What do you think made them successful?

2. Do you feel that it is important for different generations to connect with each other? Why or why not?

3. What do you feel like younger generations have to offer older generations?

4. What do you feel like older generations have to offer younger generations?

5. How can your faith community better utilize all that older and younger generations have to offer?

THE IMPORTANCE OF OLDER GENERATIONS

When I was a student at Walla Walla College (now Walla Walla University) I was a part of a group that ran a student-led worship service called Battleground. There was a church on campus called The College Church. The worship center was large and regal, with huge, vaulted ceilings. It had a pipe organ that at the time was said to have been the largest pipe organ west of Salt Lake City and north of San Francisco. Slate steps led to a large stage that could easily accommodate orchestras, choirs, etc. It was high church at its finest.

The problem was, though it was a church on a college campus, its ministry didn't seem to focus on us college students.

I'm sure there were some students who appreciated the classical music, the formal tone and pageantry associated with the College Church experience. The head pastor had thoughtful sermons and was a good storyteller. However, for many of us it lacked the relational connection and what we perceived as "real spirituality" that we craved. Battleground was our alternative.

At first, we met in a high school down the road, and then eventually moved into the college's Fine Arts Center. Lights were brought down low to minimize distraction. We had several different bands that would take turns leading worship. Speakers ranged from students to other Youth/Young Adult oriented spiritual leaders. There was an emphasis on honesty and authentic spirituality. It was packed. For many, this was the first time they had experienced church in a way that it actually affected them at a spiritual level. It also provided opportunities for students to lead in capacities where they would have never been able to in the College Church. It was a place we were proud of; a place we felt good about inviting our friends.

When my wife and I moved away, we noticed a stark contrast. We loved the church that I was working in as a pastor, but it didn't have the same sense of energy and community. The church had a lot of young families, with parents in their thirties and forties, but very few in their twenties. There were numerous times when Calista and I would express to each other how we missed the worship experience and community that Battleground had provided us.

As we address the difficulty with creating places where youth and young adults feel welcome within my own religious community, one of the options is to start another church. What about creating a "Battleground" experience? What about creating an experience that is for young adults led by young adults? I don't want to be misunderstood. I am not against this idea, and I hope it happens. There are so many positive things it could provide for the young adult community. However, I also believe that if this is all we do, we will do so at the risk of perpetuating the problem.

If creating a young adult specific church is our *only* strategy, we would essentially be admitting defeat. It would be an acknowledgement that current churches and the people in them are unable to create a healthy community. It would mean we were accepting that the generation gap is too wide, and the only alternative is a clean start where a new generation begins its journey with very minimal contact with older generations. If this is the way that things have to go to ensure the spiritual health of young adults, then so be it. Some churches will never value that part of their faith community. However, I think it is important to realize that while there are some benefits, there is also much that we would be losing.

In the last chapter we spent some time talking about the importance of young adults in a church community. For those concerned with the current disconnect between young adults and the Christian community, I think that is a relatively frequent topic of conversation. However, a community is only healthy when all members are represented. There are some important things that older generations bring that are beneficial to young adults. Let's discuss a few of those.

Older generations have wisdom from experience: There is wisdom that comes from having a few more of life's experiences under your belt. I can think back to a number of my own decisions when I was younger that if I knew what I know now, I would have made a different choice. One of my responsibilities at Camp MiVoden is to mentor the 130+ collegiate staff who work there during the summer. We hire some amazing people, many of whom go on to be leaders in our church community.[1] They are smart and talented. But as I walk with them through this portion of their life journey, there are things that they just don't know. They haven't learned some of life's lessons that can only come through experience. Failure, broken relationships, parenting, marriage, financial victories and challenges, work experience, business transactions, etc., all give us wisdom and help us with future decision making. There are few shortcuts in this process. In the context of a cross-generational connection, older generations can mentor younger generations as they navigate life's challenges.

Older generations provide stability and balance: The truth is, older generations can create chaos and imbalance just as effectively as younger generations. However, the wisdom gained through experience can help modulate their response. They don't tend to get as high or as low through life's twists and turns. When challenges arise, there is a decent chance that they have seen something like it before. They can be a valuable asset and help to channel youthful energy.

Older generations are more likely to have a healthy concept of their identity and have less to prove: As I have referenced in previous chapters, the questions of Identity, Belonging, and Value transcend generational boundaries. However, older generations are more likely to have found suitable answers to these questions. Those who have are less likely to feel like they need to prove their value to others. As they grow to understand the true source of their value, they can focus on helping others understand who they are and where their value comes from.

Older generations have time: Life for those in their 30s and 40s tends to revolve around their kids. A hectic mix of school, music lessons, karate, birthday parties, doctor's appointments, homework projects, etc., keep parents running. These generations struggle to have time for bathing, let alone leading a ministry at church. Older generations, especially those who have reached retirement, tend to have more time to invest in ministry. Connecting and mentoring younger generations can help to give them purpose in a new phase of life.

Older generations have the ability to validate younger generations in what they are doing: If you are a parent, you are well aware of the phrase "Dad (or Mom), watch this!" Kids love to show their parents things. In turn, we as parents provide validation for their efforts and encourage them. This looks a little different as we age, but the process doesn't necessarily go away. I still enjoy talking about my accomplishments with my parents. I appreciate their affirmation. In contrast, many who had dysfunctional relationships with their parents spend much of their adult lives trying to earn their approval. Older generations have the ability to validate or invalidate younger generations. The same is true in the church. If older generations come alongside younger generations to join them in their journey, celebrate their wins, and support them through their losses, it gives them confidence.

Older Generations can fund ministries: Older generations tend to be more financially stable and have more money than younger generations do. When they partner their financial abilities with the energy and creativity found in younger generations, big things can happen.

I firmly believe that if we are going to change the trajectory of the Christian church, it will be because older generations decide to bridge the gap. They will never be able to cross over to the other side. It is useless for me in my 40s to try to pretend that I am 20. Younger generations will recognize me as a fraud. However, we can still reach across the gap and make connections. In that first Youth Specialties training event I attended nearly twenty years ago, the presenter called it "sitting on the stairs to the world beneath." Other generations have created their own "world beneath" that older generations are not able to live in. But we can sit on the stairs and be a connection to the rest of the church community.

Joe

I first met Joe shortly after I moved to California. If I remember correctly, we had an initial conversation about him being involved with our youth group, and he just started showing up. To my knowledge he never taught a small group, preached a sermon, led a Bible study, acted as a worship leader, or did any of the other typical "youth leader stuff." He made it clear from the outset that his primary goal was to make sure that our teens and young adults had a chance to go on a ski trip. He showed up every week to our youth program and just "hung out." He would sit in the back and engage in the conversation, occasionally offering some good-natured heckling when appropriate. I would generally take 15 minutes before we started our small group program to listen to new bands and connect with the teens and young adults. Joe rarely missed it. He'd listen to stories, laugh at jokes, bring doughnuts, and again offer a little good-natured heckling when needed.

Joe also followed through with our annual ski trip. He contributed financially and did his best to make sure that everyone who wanted to come was able to. During the trips he would help some with logistics and assume his usual place within the group, listening to stories and offering occasional heckling. Everyone loved Joe. And Joe loved them. He had time for them and wanted to know what they were up to. He would remember what trips, events, etc. that members of our community were involved in and would ask about them when he had the opportunity.

I think Joe was in his late thirties when he started hanging out with our group. He never pretended to be in his teens or twenties. He never tried to be cool. He genuinely loved younger people and wanted to do his part to support them. He had time. He listened to stories and validated the people telling them. He wasn't perfect, but he was present and that is what mattered.

Points to Ponder

1. How do older and younger generations interact in your faith community?

2. Can you think of a time in your life when someone older did something to recognize your value? What was it? What effect did it have on you?

3. How can older generations share wisdom without appearing judgmental?

A WAY FORWARD

Have you ever reached an impasse that seemed to offer no way forward? A few months ago, I was on a surf trip with my family. It was the morning that we were supposed to pack up and return home, so I got up early for one last session. The surf was poor at the break I was planning on surfing, so I made the decision to go on a solo mission to a secret spot that is one of my favorites, but also requires about a 20 minute paddle across a shipping channel to get to. It was a beautiful sunny morning and despite my underlying fear of sharks when surfing alone (if I get hit, I at least want someone to see it), I had a great session. However, the change of location took some extra time and once I had paddled back across the channel, I was definitely trying to hurry. Typically, from where I was it took about 10-15 minutes to walk down the beach and around to the campsite, but because I was a little late on this day, I decided to take a short cut. There was a bit of a swampy marsh area with some bushes on the other side and then a road that would take me straight where I wanted to go, saving me valuable minutes.

I crossed the marsh and looked for a good spot to go through the line of bushes. There was what looked to be an animal path and I decided to take this route. Things started off easy, but gradually the bushes thickened. Branches reached out grabbing at me and my board, threatening to rip my wetsuit. As I plunged my way deeper into the undergrowth, travel became more arduous. I actually got to the point where I could see the road on the other side, but as I probed the bushes for an opening there was none. Time was ticking away, and I attacked the trek with renewed vigor, using my board to try to shield my body as I attempted to wedge my way through. Vines and branches clawed at my wetsuit, a stick poked me in the eye, and I made no progress. Eventually I was forced to retreat in defeat. I tried a couple other spots in vain, and finally had to take the walk of shame back to where I had started and down the path which I should have taken in the first place. I arrived back at camp dirty, sweaty, late, and defeated.

Sometimes I feel the same way about working for youth and young adults in ministry. For more than two decades I've battled, at times making headway, and at times retreating. There have been individual success stories. However, organizationally my faith community, and Christianity in general hasn't made much progress. What I have come to understand within my own sphere of influence is that I have been putting most of my energy into connecting with one teen or young adult at a time. This is incredibly important. However, to see change on a larger scale, I must focus on enlisting other members of my community. If I want to see organizational change, I'm going to need help. As Jesus said in Matthew 9 (NIV), "The harvest is plentiful, but the workers are few."

Keeping Young Adults in Churches

I occasionally hear people having conversations about how we can keep teens and young adults in church. The way they describe the problem is that everything is going great until they hit their teenage years, or maybe when they age out of the middle school or youth program, and then they leave. The conversation revolves around how to keep them. But young adults are leaving because they are indifferent. They are leaving because we never "had" them to begin with. Instead of building a fence to keep them in or trying to entice them with "cool stuff", a better question would be, "How do we create a community that is so irresistible that they can't stay away?"

How do we start this process with younger kids so that they are a valued part of the community all along? How do we develop a culture that intentionally integrates teens and young adults into the community in a way where they feel safe and valued? What would this kind of church look like?

Warning: Things May Change

Often when the discussion of "keeping people in church" arises, the underlying, unspoken question is "How do we make people like church the way we like it and want to be here?" We feel like if we can just flip a switch in their brain, they will realize that our way really is the best way. Maybe we add doughnuts or some other form of "progressive" ministry to help sweeten the deal. (See what I did there?)

The reality is, if we are going to truly allow younger generations to be part of our community, we have to give them some ownership. This means giving up some on our end. Church, which should be more about the community and less about the specifics of the service, will look different. The challenge is for the community to keep from alienating certain generations while at the same time maintaining cross generational connections. Much easier said than done. Give and take is important. It may even be useful for different groups to have separate classes, services, etc. to meet the spiritual needs of that segment of the community. However, the more we separate, the more we must intentionally build bridges or else the community ceases to exist.

Answering the Three Questions

I believe the key to connecting adolescents to the church community is rooted in providing answers to the three primary questions they face. These answers must be experiential, not just verbal. It involves us helping them know who they are, where they belong, and why they have value within the context of the church community. This is not just informational. We can tell them, but we must also show them through our actions. They can't just hear it. They need to experience it. Let's look at the three questions below and discuss how they fit within the context of a church community.

Who am I?

As we discussed earlier in the book, one of the primary questions of adolescence is the question of Identity. The world they live in gives them a lot of different answers to this question, all of which will eventually let them down. The ultimate reality is that we are all sons and daughters of God. This doesn't change based on our behavior. We can choose to reject this identity, but in God's eyes, even the greatest of sinners are his children. Just like the father in the story of the Prodigal Son, He will continue to offer them love and grace and welcome them into the family when they accept it. This gives all of us inherent value. Helping adolescents understand this is foundational to building an identity. This has to be reinforced through teaching and preaching. However, it also needs to be reinforced through the community offering unconditional love and grace. It doesn't mean we can't disagree or hold someone accountable. However, the way we do it will convey whether we really believe this is true.

Once the foundation is established, we can then help them understand their unique niche in the church community. Instead of centralizing our power and authority, we can look for ways to empower them and include them in areas of ministry. This doesn't mean we let them change slides in the multimedia department and call ourselves progressive. It means helping them discover their areas of interest and ability, and then putting them in positions within the church community that will assist them in using and developing their skillsets. It also means that we connect them with members in the community that can help mentor them through this process.

Where do I belong?

Many churches who hope to attract teens and young adults focus on programming. They use movie clips, contemporary music, lights, doughnuts, etc., to try to entice them to attend. They feel that if they do enough cool stuff, the institution can be awesome for Jesus, and the right people will want to come. None of these things are bad, and there are good reasons to use them in the right context. However, instead of being awesome for Jesus, we need to be loving like Jesus. We need to focus on creating a community that values youth and young adults. We need to know their story and engage in it. We also need to give them a voice. All too often the invitation to join our community really is just an invitation to be present but not an invitation to connect. We are more worried about protecting our way of worshiping and being a community than giving younger generations a seat at the table. They are welcome to attend, but they don't belong.

Churches who create belonging will not only learn their story but ask them to be a part of the community's story.

Do I matter?

Teens and young adults long to be part of something meaningful. By inviting them into leadership they get to be a part of moving God's kingdom forward here on earth. As I have had conversations with young adults over the last couple years, I have noticed an interesting trend. They are highly motivated to alleviate physical suffering, while at the same time, questioning some of the traditional ways to serve that have been offered to them. A significant portion of them are less motivated by short-term, overseas missions because they feel like showing up somewhere for a year and then leaving constitutes abandonment of the people they are serving. The same sentiment exists when they talk about door-to-door, knock-and-walk type ministries. They want to build something that is relationship based and lasting. For this group, doing something on a smaller scale with a larger and more sustained individual impact is more important than a quick strike or mass evangelism. Churches that are actively seeking to holistically meet the needs of their local community create a place where younger generations feel like they can work to build the Kingdom of God in tangible ways.

Kara Powell and Brad Griffin explore these three questions in depth, and if you are working with teens or young adults their book is definitely worth a read. In *Growing Young*, they further identify six qualities of churches who had a thriving young adult community. [1]

Unlock keychain leadership: Empower younger generations.

Empathize with today's young people: Instead of condemning, try to see through their eyes.

Take Jesus' message seriously: Don't just talk about the gospel and serving others; live it.

Fuel a warm community: Encourage warm peer and intergenerational relationships.

Prioritize young people (and families) everywhere: Support and involve them in the community.

Be the best neighbors: Enable young adults to serve locally and globally.

There is some great information in *Growing Young* as to how churches perform these tasks well. I would recommend that church leaders who are serious about implementing these strategies read this book. But what if you aren't creating church programs? What if you are just another man or woman in the church community? What is your role? I'll share my perspective on this below, but first I'd like to tell you about Rick and Murry.

Rick and Murry

Rick and Murry (not their real names) are a father-son duo that attend the same church that I do. Murry is a retired pastor and bona fide cowboy. He's been known to run up front unprompted and whirl about with an honest to goodness sling if someone sings "Only A Boy Named David." (I'm pretty sure he keeps that thing in his pocket at all times.) His son Rick works in tech and has been a mainstay at my church for decades. Rick and Murry love people. For as long as they have been a part of our community, they could always be seen before and after church connecting with people.

A number of years back, these two decided to get intentional about helping people establish relationships in the church community. They began working with the greeting teams and set themselves up in the entryway between the scheduled greeters and our community breakfast ministry. Once guests had moved past the official greeters in the entryway, Rick and Murry would introduce themselves. They would learn each guest's story, and then personally connect them with a more regular attender with whom they had something in common. Stories began to come in about people who visited our church and never left because of how "friendly" we were and how they were able to connect to the community. They weren't able to connect everyone, but the impact was substantial.

A number of years later, the COVID pandemic hit. Our church, like most others, was challenged during that time as we have strong representation on both sides of the political spectrum in our religious community, as well as within our leadership team. We shut down for a couple of brief periods and had to put our community breakfast ministry on hold for a time as well. During these months we began to see less of Rick and Murry for a few different reasons that are not important for this conversation. Things rebounded and the church became busy again. The breakfast ministry returned, and our numbers began to return to what they were before the pandemic. However, Rick and Murry did not return to their prior ministry. I began to hear stories about people coming and no one but the pastor speaking to them. It was during this time that the friends I referenced earlier in the book came, visited, and were disappointed. I began to hear a shift in the narrative that floated around in the greater community from people talking about how our church was one of the most friendly in the area, to one that could tend to be cliquish and unfriendly.

I think it is important to recognize that the COVID experience changed a lot of things and created barriers between people that didn't exist before. For years our church was known for being a place where conservatives and liberals with vastly different views on religion and politics could sit and enjoy breakfast together. This value was severely challenged. Even now we are growing, but are still recovering from our wounds. However, I believe that there was a significant shift in experience, especially for people who were not already connected to our community, when we lost our two-man networking crew. These guys aren't perfect. They are flawed humans like the rest of us. But they both recognized the need for people to be connected to the community and didn't let themselves be controlled by the fears that typically keep us from reaching out.

As I have been pondering these ideas over the last couple years, the thought has crossed my mind more than once. What if we didn't just have Rick and Murry? What if we had 10 people like them? What if we had 100?

One Bridge at a Time

I believe the key to connecting younger generations to our community isn't a program or finding just the right youth leaders. Being intentional is important, but the only way to span the generation gap is to build one bridge at a time. We need a lot of bridge builders. But there are many barriers to bridge building. In earlier chapters we noted that fear created by our own search for value gets in the way. Once we make sense of that, there are still inherent challenges created by the generation gap that can limit our effectiveness.

Become One Who Sees

I have a friend named Eric. Eric is a survival expert. Not a survival expert like your Uncle Wally who once tried to suck the venom out of a garter snake bite and gets a fire started every time with his blow torch. Eric is the real deal. He has spent years honing his craft, including attending Tom Brown Jr's Tracking School, based on the teachings of Stalking Wolf (best name ever!), an Apache who began passing on his knowledge to Tom when he was seven years old. Every time we get a chance to hang out in a wilderness setting–which doesn't happen often enough–my mind is blown.

Every year our church hosts an event called Forged. It is a weekend for men who don't go to retreats. It is amazing. Part of what makes it amazing is that Eric agrees to teach us some of his skills. A couple years ago I asked him to demonstrate the art of camouflage. When he is teaching survival skills, he has a game he likes to do with his students where he helps a few of them prepare themselves and hide within six feet of the road or trail. Then the rest of the group walks by and tries to find them. They usually don't.

This time Eric and his brother Matt were both at the event, and at my request, they agreed to hide Matt at the next meeting in the MiVoden Campfire Bowl, an amphitheater with a stage and gravel terraced wood benches. He would be camouflaged but not covered. He would be in plain sight. I was skeptical.

A half hour before the meeting, Eric told me that he was going to help Matt prep and indicated where he would be hiding. However, as I walked into the amphitheater, there seemed to be a mistake. Matt was nowhere to be seen. I was about to go and ask Eric if he had decided to do it at another meeting, when I noticed an anomaly on the ground off to the side of one of the benches. There was what appeared to be a pile of rubbish, with about 25 pine needles sprinkled over the top in the place where his brother was supposed to be. Men were hanging around, stepping over and around this odd shape, never giving a second thought to the form laying in plain sight near their feet.

We started the meeting with about 60 guys present, and I invited Eric to the stage. He announced that his brother was hidden in the Campfire Bowl and instructed the guys to look around and see if they could find him. About 10% found him. Next, he invited them to walk around and indicated which half of the amphitheater he was hidden in. Probably 50% of them found him. Finally, he indicated a narrow section of about 20 x 40 feet. There were still probably 10-15 guys that never saw him until he moved.

The amazing thing about this demonstration is that Matt wasn't hiding under anything. His clothes were earth tones and then rubbed with dirt. His face was strategically painted, a few pine needles, sticks and leaves were strategically placed on him, but he was in plain sight. I would have never believed it if I hadn't seen it, or not seen it, with my own eyes. It made my brain hurt trying to process what I had just witnessed. How could a grown man be sitting in plain sight, and yet not be seen?

And yet there are thousands of people who attend churches every week who are unseen. They aren't hiding, they are in plain sight, and yet they go unnoticed. Or maybe they are noticed, but only as a pile of rubbish to avoid running into, but not recognized for the child of God that they are. They may be young or old. However, when they are outside of our generation, it can make them less visible to us. Or maybe we see them, but they are so different from us that we struggle to recognize their humanity.

The first step in connecting across generational divides is to learn to see people differently, or sometimes to learn to see them at all. Churches tend to be communities that are made up of multiple smaller communities who live and worship in parallel experiences that rarely ever intersect. This means that we may go to a church with hundreds or thousands of people, but only have meaningful interaction with a small portion of that community. Even small churches often experience this dynamic. In order to become a warm, loving community we need to be able to see beyond our group of friends and create intentional interactions with those not already in our circle. In doing this we recognize their inherent value.

Become One Who Listens

Have you ever had a conversation with someone and realized halfway through that they aren't paying any attention to what you are saying? I have, and I know my wife has. (Sorry Calista!) My son Reef and I had one such conversation this morning when I asked him to wake up his sister to get ready for school. I was headed out for a workout (this "dad bod" doesn't happen by accident) and I wasn't going to be back in time to make sure she woke up to get ready for school. Before I left, I went up to Reef's room and told him that I needed him to wake her up at 7:00. He said he would, but I wasn't convinced. "Reef," I said, "I need you to make sure you get her up, so she has enough time. Do you understand?" He assured me that he did, and I headed out.

Too much sweat and too few calories later, I returned to the house at around 7:20, with a ten-minute cushion till our departure time. As I walked in the front door, I immediately became concerned. Things were too quiet. The usual morning soundtrack emanating several decibels too loud from my daughter's room was not present. I headed down the hallway and my fears were confirmed when I found her sleeping serenely, her dog Jag and cat Sunshine still snuggled soundly in place. The next 10 minutes were a whirlwind of lunch prep, hygiene (or the lack thereof), and some fine motivational speaking on my part to get her loaded up and headed for school.

When I asked Reef about our earlier conversation, he had zero recollection of it taking place. It wasn't that he was trying to get out of it, he just never heard. His mind was focused on something else, and his responses were reflexive as opposed to indicative of any comprehension. This pattern isn't surprising; there is a genetic component involved. (He gets it from his mother? Guess again.) But it is an excellent example of speaking without communicating, hearing without listening.

For many people, starting a conversation with someone new is the scary part. How does one initiate contact? What should we say? What if they think we are weird or pushy? This is where we are tempted to revert to being "Awesome for Jesus" or to flee in terror. Oftentimes we are so worried about our contribution to the conversation that we don't actually hear what they are saying. We are too busy thinking about the next story or joke we are going to tell, what our hair or clothes look like, or who we are going to talk to next that we miss our chance to listen.

I've found it important in my experience to continue to remind myself that ministry is about me showing other people that they are valuable, not proving my own worth. The best way to do this is to listen to their story. If initiating conversations is challenging for you, it may be helpful to have some questions in your back pocket to get their story started. The following are good areas to explore.

Hometown

- "Tell me about where you are from."

- "Are you from this area?"

- "What are some of the things that you love about this area?"

School

- "Where are you going to school?" ("Where did you go if recently graduated?")

- "What is your school like?"

- "Are you involved in any programs?" (sports, art, music, etc.)

Job

- "Where do you work?"

- "What are some of the things you love about working there?"

Hobbies

- "What are some of your favorite things to do? "

Food

- "What are some of your favorite places to eat around here?"

- "If I go there, what should I order? What is your favorite dish?"

Once the conversation is started, then just be curious. Asking questions about someone's life experiences is much easier when we actually take an interest in them. Make it your goal to learn more about who they are and affirm them in that.

"I've never heard of anything like that. Tell me more."

"That sounds really fun! How did you get into it?"

"What attracted you about working there?"

"That sounds challenging. How did you learn to deal with it?"

Be careful with topics such as religion and politics as they can easily become divisive. Also be careful with compliments. You don't want to be creepy or push them toward a production-based sense of self-worth. Look for areas of shared experience and acknowledge them. Be careful to avoid taking over the story when you find areas of common interest.

"That's so cool that you love to ski. Me too. I used to be a racer you know…"

Once the conversation is finished, thank them for sharing part of their story and let them know you look forward to talking again sometime. Then do your best to remember their name next time you see them. (Good luck! I'm awful at that part.) When we know someone's name, they become more than just another member of the crowd. Acknowledging them by name lets them know that you see them. Just greeting them by name in passing shows that you noticed them, and you value their presence.

Seeing and listening are the basics of being a warm and welcoming community. If most of us would just do that, it would revolutionize our churches. I believe that this alone would change the way that younger generations and older generations see the church.

Become One Who Engages

Engaging in someone's story goes a step beyond seeing and listening. A group of seeing and listening people has the ability to completely transform how their community is perceived. However, if our ministry is driven by the love and grace that we have experienced in our own lives, it is likely that we won't be content to just listen to the stories of others. We will feel drawn to engage, to join their story with the purpose of seeing them experience love and grace in their own life.

For some this may be as simple as following up on their story at another time.

"Hey Liz, I remember you told me a couple weeks ago about a road trip you were going to take with a group of friends. How was that?"

If you remember, there is a ratio that tends to be true with human relationships. (150:15:5) They may not be a part of your 5 or 15. You shouldn't feel like they have to be. But casual interactions within the community are still important. They keep us connected and still impart value. We are also more easily guided by the Holy Spirit when a ministry need arises. Needs are more easily recognized, and we may even be called to speak truth into someone's life. Without a pre-existing relationship, we have not earned the right, nor will we have the insight to interact in more meaningful ways.

There are some people with whom you may feel called to engage in a deeper way. They may become a part of your 15, or even your 5. If you are reaching across generational divides, you may be called to engage with someone in a mentoring type of relationship. These types of interactions have the ability to be life changing for both mentor and mentee. Yet for many of us the idea can be a bit unnerving. The same internal voices that told us we weren't awesome enough to talk to them in the first place now tell us that we don't have anything to offer. We are afraid we won't know what to say. Maybe we don't have enough wisdom. Then there are others who are packed full of "wisdom" and ready to explode. They will vomit wisdom and "Awesomeness for Jesus" all over their unsuspecting mentee. In truth, being a mentor is really just taking your listening to the next level, being curious, and coming alongside your mentee in their life journey.

Points to Ponder

1. How might your faith community benefit teens and young adults who are searching for answers regarding identity, belonging, and autonomy?

2. Do you have any people in your faith community like Rick and Murray? What do you think makes them successful at connecting with people? What would happen in your faith community if you had 10 people with the same focus as Rick and Murray? What if you had 100 people with that focus?

3. What could be done in your faith community to enlist more bridge builders?

4. What barriers do you recognize in your experiences

that keeps you from being someone who sees, listens, and engages? What could you do to remove some of them?

MENTORING 101

I'm a big Seattle Seahawks fan. This didn't just start when they won the Superbowl in 2013 as it did for many. I was a fan long before they were good. I was a fan when the refs lost them their first Super Bowl to the Pittsburgh Steelers in 2006. I was also a fan when the refs gave them a win over the Green Bay Packers in 2012 with the infamous "Fail Mary." (We're probably even now.) I have been a fan through thick and thin. My family also joins me in my fandom. My wife Calista even has a signed Steve Largent football from when she was a kid.

Growing up in the Pacific Northwest, Seattle teams have always been "my teams." However, there is something that connects me to the Seahawks beyond their proximity to my location. I'm fascinated by their coach Pete Carrol.

Pete Carroll is an anomaly in the NFL coaching world. In a world where it is generally believed that being hard and angry begets toughness, Pete stands out with his overwhelming positivity. Some coaches are known for their creative play calling. Others use fear and intimidation to motivate their players to do their best. Pete Carroll's secret weapon is his culture. One of the first things that players notice when they show up for a Pete Carroll practice is the atmosphere. The music is cranked up. There are crazy games and competitions that have nothing to do with football. There are pranks and tomfoolery. It is extremely competitive, but with an atmosphere where each player is uplifted and encouraged to be their best.

When describing his philosophy, Pete says, "Each person holds so much power within themselves that needs to be let out. Sometimes they just need a little nudge, a little direction, a little support, a little coaching, and the greatest things can h appen."[1] He believes that players will be most successful in an environment where they feel valued. He and his coaches spend their time learning how to interact with each player in order to unlock their maximum potential. He and the general manager John Schneider are known for taking players that have not done well in other environments, who may have issues off the field that have impacted their ability to perform, and helping them realize their true potential. While others in the league may label these players as lost causes, Pete sees them differently. "People make mistakes all the time. We learn and grow. If there's patience and love, and you care for people, you can work them through it, and they can find their greatest heights. It comes down to taking care of the people in your program and making them the best they can be, not giving up on them and never failing to be there for them."[2]

The interesting thing about Pete is that he failed out in his first job as a head coach in the NFL in 1994 with the New York Jets. He also spent some time with the New England Patriots in the late 1990s before making the switch to college football with the University of Southern California, where he revived their struggling football program. Despite a rocky start and a controversial exit, his tenure at USC was incredibly successful.

In 2010 he left the program to become the coach of the Seattle Seahawks, this time bringing along much of what he had learned about creating a successful program in college to the NFL. "I wanted to find out if we went to the NFL and really took care of guys, really cared about each and every individual, what would happen?"[3] This focus on connecting with and mentoring players piloted the Seahawks to their first Superbowl win and more than a decade as one of the top teams in the NFL. But Pete's leadership goes beyond football. He helps facilitate conversations about life and social justice within his community. He continues to relentlessly pursue ways to help the young men on his team grow and to advocate for player rights, especially when it comes to dealing with injuries. "I would say that we have to explore and find ways to make our game a better game and take care of our players in whatever way possible. Regardless of what other stigmas might be involved, we have to do this because the world of medicine is doing this."

Pete Carroll gets the best from his players, because he wants the best for his players.

The thing that intrigues me about Pete's approach is that there are so many religious undertones. He emphasizes grace and helping players understand their value. His focus is on understanding each one and helping them find their place in the Seahawks football community. He is willing to change the application of his philosophy (not the philosophy itself) to match the individual strengths and weaknesses of his players. It sounds so much like successful youth and young adult ministry. Even when his players lash out at him or talk bad about him and his philosophy, he doesn't retaliate. He is confident in his own identity, which allows him to respond to his players with grace and support.

I don't know much about Pete's religious beliefs. One website describes his faith as a blend of Methodist-Episcopal with Zoroastrianism, but I couldn't find much else to confirm that.[4] While I'm sure we would differ on some points of theology, I am amazed at how he has been able to take the concepts of mentorship and grace and apply it to an industry that is built on competition and survival of the fittest. What's more, Pete is the oldest coach in the NFL at over 70 years old. If it can work in the pro football community, think of what it could accomplish in the church, a community built on love, grace, and the value of people.

A Few Mentoring Basics

Mentoring is not all that complex. However, because it is so uncommon in our society, many of us don't have a clue on how to start. Despite mentoring youth and young adults for decades, I am still growing in my understanding and abilities. I am not an expert, but I have experienced some success. Below are some mentoring basics that I have found useful over the years.

Quality over quantity: Don't try to mentor everyone. You can't do it, and you shouldn't. Ask God to guide you in deciding who you are called to connect with in this way. You will be more effective and have emotional energy left over for the other people in your life.

Establish a relationship: Don't try to hop right into people's lives and give them advice. You earn the right to speak truth to people by building a relationship. Even then it is important to move forward with humility. People will usually ask for your thoughts if they want to hear them. In the words of Dr. David Thomas, my former advisor in my theology program at Walla

Walla University, "Advice is generally worth what you pay for it." You probably aren't as smart as you think you are.

Show Empathy: When people tell us their stories it is easy to make assumptions, come to a snap judgment, and jump into fix-it mode. Often what people really need is for someone to feel a little bit of what they are feeling. To understand the stress, sadness, anger, loneliness, etc. they are dealing with. Showing empathy is one of the most effective ways that we can show others they are valuable to us. It is better to acknowledge their emotions and experience, than to launch into a story about how something similar happened to you once, and how you overcame it.

Develop Trust: Trust is not a right, and typically does not happen overnight. If we try to dig into people's lives before we have developed adequate trust, we tend to push them away. They have defenses for a reason. They aren't going to open up to you until they know that you are safe. Typically, they will start by sharing smaller, less consequential parts of themselves. If we handle these well, they will gradually be more willing to be vulnerable. It is important that mentors maintain integrity and confidentiality. (Unless they or someone else is in danger. More about that in a bit.)

Be vulnerable and humble: Modeling vulnerability is a major part of trust. Don't spill all of your deep dark secrets right up front. However, being vulnerable with your own life experiences gives them permission to be more open with theirs. It gives them a chance to see some of their own story within yours. Humility is a must with any relationship.

Ask questions instead of giving answers: One of the aspects of mentoring that many new, and even experienced mentors find challenging is learning how to ask questions. If we are in a mentoring role, it is likely that we tend to be problem fixers. As we listen and attempt to engage in someone's story, our natural inclination is to give them the answer. However, this is generally not the best strategy. Effective mentors learn how to use questions to help their mentee explore the issue and find the answer. This doesn't mean we can't ever give advice. However, we are usually much too quick to jump in and provide a "solution" instead of walking through the process with them.

Guide them in seeking a Godly solution: When it is time to really dig for a solution, one of the ways we can help our mentees find the best way forward is to ask questions that encourage them to seek a Godly solution. Despite calling themselves Christians, many people have a hard time incorporating their faith into their daily life experience and decision making. Questions such as, "How do you see God working in this situation?", "What do you feel like God's response to your pain is?", and "Where do you think God is leading you next?" encourage mentees to consider the spiritual dimension when looking for a solution. As they grow in their understanding of what it means to be a son or daughter of God, we want to help them start to make this reality the center of their decision-making process.

Celebrate Milestones: As western culture has evolved, many of the milestones of growing into adulthood have gone by the wayside. Jewish culture is full of ceremonies that reinforce identity, belonging, and the path to adulthood. Bar Mitzvah/Bat Mitzvah ceremonies celebrate an adolescent moving into adulthood. Festivals such as Yom Kippur and Passover reinforce their history, place in the community, and connection to God. If we look at Native American cultures, there were specific steps and ceremonies that took place in order for an adolescent to become an adult man or woman. Tribe elders would mentor them through this process, but also provide the freedom for self-discovery. Many ancient cultures had a very specific process to becoming an adult. However, as these cultures become more westernized, they tend to lose these parts of the adolescent journey. Young adults tend to be left on their own to figure out what it means to grow up. The rest of the community watches from the sidelines, making occasional comments about how they are doing it wrong.

Slow Down: Recently our MiVoden team has been reading a book entitled *The Ruthless Elimination of Hurry*[5]. The book is built around one central theme: Love is incompatible with hurry. As I look at my own life, hurry is the biggest barrier to mentoring and other types of ministry. The drive to get things done often overpowers the prompting of the Holy Spirit, gently nudging me to stop and listen to someone. Unless we create time and space in our hectic lives, we will miss out on journeying with the people around us. Busyness is not Godliness.

Intentionally Create Time for Shared Experiences: Because we tend to live life at such a frantic pace, it is important to schedule opportunities for shared experiences. These can be recreational opportunities, service projects, meeting for coffee, etc. Even more structured activities can be an opportunity for shared experience. A couple of years ago during summer camp we had a more experienced staff leadership team. Within a few weeks these young adults were dialed in and operating a tight ship. With the program running smoothly, we decided to discontinue our weekly leadership meetings. We still had a brief daily check-in with the team (though we began to skip some of these as well) but not our weekly, more in depth, late night gatherings. For a while everything continued to run smoothly, and the leadership team was grateful for a few more hours of rest. However, we gradually began to see breakdowns in relationships and frustration began to build. Thankfully we recognized what was happening and revived our meetings before relationships were too fractured. This experience drove home the importance of togetherness, not just because we could take care of business, but also because it created opportunities to communicate and support each other. We needed intentional time to connect and maintain relationships.

Offer Grace: Lists don't change people. Grace does. We live in a world that is often devoid of grace. You may be the first person to show your mentee that they are valuable, in spite of their mistakes.

Don't Be One Who Destroys

Before I leave the topic of mentoring, it is important to recognize that there are risks for both mentor and mentee. There are some who will use these types of relationships for their own personal gain and gratification. There are others who have really good intentions, but a lack of awareness causes them to make a poor decision that is unhealthy for one or both of them. There are other resources where you can explore the nuances of mentorship, but here are a few areas that deserve extra care to avoid harming yourself or the person you are mentoring.

Avoid inappropriate relationships or the appearance of them: Don't engage in any kind of flirtatious or romantic mentor-mentee interactions. Don't meet alone in clandestine locations. Do meet in public places, or in rooms with windows where you can be observed by others. Be very careful with hugs and other physical contact. We live in a world where many people have experienced things they never should have had to experience. Our goal is to spread love and grace, not to harm. While both parties should make wise decisions, it is the role of the mentor to make sure that interactions are done in a healthy way.

Dangerous secrets: Be careful with secrets. Confidentiality is one of the base building blocks of a mentor-mentee relationship. However, there are situations where confidentiality has to be broken to avoid harm. If someone's life is in danger, if someone is being abused in some way, or if a crime is being committed, these are situations where professionals need to be involved. If someone is dealing with mental illness, especially if they are talking about suicide, they need more help than you can give them. In most cases it is wise to involve them in the decision to seek help. Maybe inviting them to go with you to talk to someone. However, there are times when the hard decisions must be made. It is the duty of the mentor to recognize these situations and do the hard thing.

Don't be a hero: There have been occasions in my experience as a youth pastor when I have worked with teens and young adults who were really struggling. I've sat in the emergency room with a mentee as they recover from severe alcohol poisoning. I've gone and picked up mentees and extracted them from some rough situations. I've taken calls at all times of the day from those struggling with addiction, contemplating suicide, or experiencing grief or depression. I am honored to be the one they called when they were at the end of their rope. However, there have also been times when I have abandoned my family to deal with things that were not urgent. There have been times when I should have let mentees know when I was available and when I was not. Setting boundaries can be difficult, but it is important. Not only is it healthier for you, but it will also model healthy mentorship for your mentee, who may one day be in your shoes.

Being a mentor is an incredibly gratifying experience. My friend Jon had a mentor tell him that as adults we should all seek out someone half our age to mentor, and someone twice our age to mentor us. Obviously, this gets a little more difficult when we are at the younger and the older end of the spectrum. However, the point is a good one. All of us have something to offer others. All of us will benefit from spending time with someone who, in turn, has something to offer us.

Points to Ponder

1. Has there been anyone in your life who acted as a mentor? Who were they and what did they do that made an impression on your life?

2. Are you a mentor or mentee for someone in your faith community right now? How could you be more intentional about maximizing the benefits from that

relationship for both parties?

3. How could your faith community become better at mentoring teens and young adults?

4. What would it take for you to be willing to be a mentor?

THE FINAL INGREDIENT

Zholia Alemi, a "psychiatrist" in England was recently sent to prison. She had worked for over 20 years as a physician, at times employed by England's National Health Service, as well as a number of health bodies and trusts. She had treated hundreds of patients and worked in a number of hospitals across England, Wales and Scotland. Her earnings allowed her to purchase multiple properties, collect expensive champagne and drive a red Lotus. The problem was, she wasn't a real doctor. Alemi had attended the University of Auckland in New Zealand and began the six-year medical training but had failed out after completing a small portion of the degree. She moved to England in 1995 and worked as a housekeeper for a bit before obtaining a Commonwealth Medical License by sending in forged documents.

Alemi practiced medicine for nearly 20 years without arousing suspicion until 2017 when she was taken to court for allegedly forging the will of one of her patients. She had befriended the 84-year-old widow and would help her with day-to-day activities. An investigation into the terms of her patient's will after the woman died showed that nearly all of the 1.3 million pound estate had been taken by Alemi and sent to her grandchildren in the United States. She was found guilty of fraud and sent to prison for 5 years.

The matter would have ended there if it weren't for the curiosity of a reporter by the name of Phil Coleman. He couldn't understand someone in her position committing this crime and decided to investigate further. As he dug, he found inconsistencies with her verification documents from the University of Auckland and eventually discovered that she had never actually graduated. Police discovered further incriminating documentation when they searched one of her homes, including a forged official "Letter of varification". (Your friend who always corrects your spelling will get it if you don't.) In February of 2023 she was found guilty of 13 counts of fraud, three counts of obtaining a pecuniary advantage by deception, two counts of forgery, and two counts of using a false instrument. She was sentenced to seven years in prison for what the judge described as a "deliberate and wicked deception."[1] [2]

Don't Be a Kook

In 2001 I spent a semester studying at Avondale University in Australia. My girlfriend (now wife) Calista had gone down at the beginning of the year, and a couple of buddies and I decided to join her for the second semester. It was great to see her, and I was able to continue to work toward my degree, but there was one other thing that enticed my friends and me to travel down under: we wanted to learn to surf. Our first day there we bought a car, bought surfboards, and headed to the beach. I think I surfed five days a week while I was there, and surfing continues to be one of my favorite forms of recreation to this day. Despite living 7-8 hours from the closest beach, I continue to check the conditions regularly, have made a few of my own boards, swim weekly to stay in shape, and make monthly pilgrimages to the coast. I'm not an expert, but I am still obsessed with the ocean and waves. (My wife refuses to let me drive when we are near the ocean on family trips because she is worried I will drive off the road while looking for waves.)

While I was in Australia, I noticed an interesting phenomenon with some of my fellow students. Surf culture was huge in Australia. Professional surfers there were treated by the general public with much of the same devotion as we in the United States might treat football or basketball athletes. Upon returning from a surf session, I was often engaged by fellow students who asked how the waves were. They wanted to know which beach I surfed, what the tides were like, and the size of the swell.

Occasionally they would recommend beaches that I should try on my next session. They wore surf-style clothing and used surfing terms effectively in conversation. However, when I would invite them to join me on my next adventure, they would decline and respond with, "Oh, I don't surf."

To be fair, there were some really talented surfers that went to school there and were just as obsessed as I was. Yet, a surprising number of people looked like surfers, sounded like surfers, conversed like surfers, but never paddled out into the waves.

People aren't always what they appear to be. In surfing they are called Kooks. Other names in the sporting world are Jerrys, Gapers, Posers, etc. In business when someone isn't what they are supposed to be they are frauds. In religion, we call them hypocrites. This actually comes from the Greek term *Hypokrites* which refers to "an actor" or "a stage player."[3] It is a compound of words that literally translates to "an interpreter from underneath." *Hypokrites* in Greek theater wore large masks to mark the characters they played, so acting was their interpretation of the character the mask represented. It involved them adopting the mannerisms, language, etc., of their character to help the audience connect with it while at the same time hiding their true identity.

Before I continue, I think it is important to recognize that all of us demonstrate some level of hypocrisy. It is impossible for our outward self to completely match who we are inwardly.

We all make decisions on occasion that aren't consistent with our character and values. Some of us struggle with it more than others, but it is a universal condition. We are all guilty of being kooks. Matters of faith and spirituality are frequently the context within which our kookdom thrives. This isn't about judgment and condemnation. Christians aren't perfect. That is what grace is for.

But there is something that I believe makes our inconsistencies far more dangerous and destructive. It's one thing to be a kook. It is another to be one but believe that you aren't. In surfing it can get you into dangerous situations and ruin the surfing experience for others. Surfers at Pipeline in Oahu and other high profile, high consequence breaks have developed a culture and way of controlling who paddles out. Locals will verbally, and sometimes physically regulate the line-up. While "localism" can be frustrating for other surfers and, quite frankly, often comes from selfish motivations, it also serves the purpose of keeping the line-up safe. Pipeline is a highly dangerous wave that has taken multiple lives. Beginner, intermediate, and many advanced surfers are not skilled enough to manage the challenges and risks of this break. They would not only be a danger to themselves but also put other surfers in harm's way.

In religion being a kook at best renders us less effective, and at worst can do serious damage to the people around us. If we know that we are being hypocritical, it isn't healthy, but we also know there is something better. We know that we aren't living up to our values and beliefs. We are much less likely to be satisfied with our current condition. However, if we don't realize that what we say we believe doesn't add up with the way we actually live our lives, then we feel like we are good where we are. We may even feel more spiritual and like we are "fighting sin" when in actuality we are working against what God is doing in our community. There are a number of areas in our religious experience where this tends to be applicable. I'm going to be a little vulnerable about an area that challenges me in my spiritual journey, but that I also think is an important part of being successful in creating a community that teens, young adults, and people of all ages are drawn to.

I am a rule follower. Ever since I was young, I have always done my best to do the right thing. Whether with religion, the government, a job, etc. I tend toward making a concerted effort to do it the way it is supposed to be done. If the line at the cafeteria says to take one cookie, I take one cookie. (Incidentally, I married someone who believes that rules were meant to be broken, which has led to numerous, and at times spirited debates.) This combines with a value system that tends to emphasize production. At my core, I can sometimes be a little legalistic. I like to break things down to a formula.

Prayer + Bible Study + Serving Others – Doing bad stuff = Good Christian.

It is easier to track. I feel like I am doing something. I understand that I am saved by grace, but I tend to evaluate my spiritual journey on the things that I am doing or accomplishing. I feel more spiritual when I am doing good things.

I don't do well with inactivity. I don't do well with silence. I don't do well with listening. I struggle to focus, to quiet my mind, to create time and space for God to communicate with me. I would much rather be "doing something" than trying to connect with God on a spiritual level. When I pray, I have a list of things that I talk to God about. However, when I try to listen for a response, my mind wanders. I have had some amazing moments of real spiritual connection, but much of my spiritual experience tends to be solely knowledge-based. I know a lot about God but struggle to create the dynamics for a relational connection. In my work as a pastor, I have often found that I would much rather write a sermon than spend time connecting with the God I am writing about. I use good works as a cop-out for spiritual connection. What makes it worse is that church communities love people like me. When we see someone "producing" a lot, they are seen as the spiritual champions of the community. I'm not saying I'm anyone's hero. I'm just acknowledging what we tend to value.

For many years, I didn't recognize that this was a problem. I felt just fine being at that stage of spiritual development, and at times felt a little smug and superior regarding those who didn't have things together like me. (There was still darkness in my life that I just chose to push aside most of the time.) I didn't realize that I was a "spiritual kook" because I was substituting works for true spiritual connection. I could talk about a friendship with God, but in reality, it was more religiosity than relationship. I don't think God was mad at me. And I don't think I was playing for the wrong team. It isn't as though I was not a follower of God. However, I also believe that my emphasis on works at the detriment of a true spiritual connection at times has limited my effectiveness in ministry and robbed me of peace. How can I be led by the Holy Spirit when my primary focus is on me having my stuff together? How can I show other people that they are valuable when I am working to build my own religious value?

It Isn't Primarily a Knowledge Problem

In this book I have shared a lot of knowledge. There have been statistics and "how-tos" regarding building relationships with people. However, I don't think our issues tend to be primarily a knowledge problem. Sure, understanding more about how communities and even how our own minds work is definitely helpful. But if we want to truly be a community that spreads love and grace, we have to create time and space for God to connect with us. We have to listen and be guided by the Holy Spirit. This doesn't happen by accident. Unless we create opportunities for connection with God–on purpose–we'll be lacking in this part of our experience.

It is really no different than in our human relationships. If my connection with my wife consists only of me knowing that she likes fast cars, is excellent at her job, dislikes onions, and does not tolerate loud noises regardless of their origin or how incredibly exciting the moment is, but I don't actually spend any quality time connecting with her, our marriage is probably not going to survive. It doesn't necessarily matter how much I know about God. The Bible tells me that demons have all of this information too. "You believe that there is one God. Good! Even the demons believe that—and shudder." James 2:19. NIV

Another way to articulate the type of belief in Christ that is life-changing and leads to salvation is *trust*. To trust is to know information and make decisions that require vulnerability based on this knowledge from the past. It means we believe that God is love and order our life around this concept. Christians often talk about belief in informational terms. I need to know the right things about God to obtain salvation. However, James tells us that knowledge doesn't lead to a friendship with God. Information is only helpful when it leads to a relational connection. In our society when someone knows a lot of information about someone but has no relationship with them, we call them a fan...or a stalker. In some ways I feel like many of us are spiritual stalkers.

Before Jesus returned to heaven, He had a final sit down with his disciples. In Acts 1, Jesus tells them over dinner that they are not to leave Jerusalem but wait for the gift that the Father had promised. Verse 8 (NIV) says, "But you will receive power when the Holy Spirit comes on you; and you will be my witnesses in Jerusalem, and in all Judea and Samaria, and to the ends of the earth." Immediately after that Jesus returns to heaven, and they are left alone. These men (and women) have been with Jesus, heard every word He has said, seen His death and resurrection, and they aren't ready yet. They don't know what to do. In fact, two heavenly messengers have to tell them to quit gawking at the sky and move forward. They haven't received the power. All they can do is wait.

Just like we discussed regarding Peter in previous chapters, they had all spent time with Jesus. They knew stuff. They had first-hand knowledge. But their hearts had not been transformed. It wasn't till they waited, and they prayed, and they listened that they created the time and space for the Holy Spirit to change them. And change them He did! They went from hiding in a room together, timid and afraid, to starting a fire that changed the course of history.

There is an interesting thing that Christians say sometimes that shows how hard it is for us to grasp this concept. People talk about Christians who "have Jesus's love in their hearts and don't share it". It's almost as if they have taken the gospel hostage for themselves but are too selfish to share it with anybody else. But here's the thing, if you are "keeping the gospel to yourself" it is likely that you are not actually experiencing it yourself. You may be able to describe the experience, and you may even be able to convince yourself that you are living a life driven by it. But when we create time and space to truly experience the love and goodness God has for us, we can't hold it in, or we will explode. At one point, Jesus said the very rocks and trees would cry out if people held it in!

Part of the reason I feel that in general churches are shrinking is that we have become good at walking, talking, dressing, and eating like Christians, but are more challenged at actually connecting on a spiritual and relational level with the God we are following. We have resorted to trying to build the kingdom of God with power, money, strategic planning, political lobbying, showmanship, intentional programming, etc.

I don't write this to shame you into reading your Bible more, to guilt you into doing "loving" things. My hope is that all of us, including myself, will be able to recognize what we are missing. Being a fan is great. We can spout facts, name drop a bit, and talk about the one time that we saw our favorite celebrity, or someone that looked like them, on a plane. But what if instead of just knowing about someone, we were actually friends? What if that happened with God?

I believe that this is the first step into finding our way forward. The Body of Christ still needs all parts, and all parts need the body. The Christian community has so much to offer people of all ages when it is rooted in the Gospel. This book is an invitation. It is a call to see people differently. A call to see yourself differently. A call to see God differently. Start with the lens of grace, discover where your true value comes from, and then allow yourself to become the "new creation" that Paul talks about in 2 Corinthians 5. Allow yourself to begin to see the world through God's eyes and let the love and grace that you have experienced in your own life begin to flow out to the people around you.

Some have asked me what all of this looks like practically. This is a little tougher to answer. Not because it is a difficult concept, but because it will look different for each person. Instead of a list of ideas and concepts, here are some examples.

Summer Camp

When I was in college, I spent four of my summers working at Camp MiVoden. I never attended camp when I was younger but was there with my family for some teacher's meetings at the end of one summer and went wakeboarding with some of the waterfront staff. I was good enough that they encouraged me to apply and the following summer I was the wakeboard camp boy's counselor/instructor.

Camp life was amazing and also challenging. The hours were long. I was put into positions of responsibility that I was probably not quite ready for. I was responsible for not only making sure that my campers survived, but also for helping them coexist in a positive way (i.e., not fighting), providing discipline when necessary, giving evening devotions, and teaching them what I knew about following Jesus. I also had amazing conversations about life, love, and religion with other staff members, and moments of mentoring by some of the older members of the camp community. Camp was a place that I knew I belonged, where I had a purpose, and there was a culture that helped me begin to understand who I was in Christ.

I remember one instance when I was hauling a boat trailer up to our parking area when suddenly I noticed a strange phenomenon. The boat trailer was growing smaller and smaller in my rearview mirror. By the time I got the truck stopped and jumped out of the cab, the trailer–which was separated from the truck–was headed down the hill backwards at a pretty good clip. Fortunately, being the consummate athlete that I was, I was able to run the trailer down, grab the tongue, and turn it into the bank before things got too out of hand. Right about that time my supervisor came strolling around the corner, saw my plight, chuckled a bit, and helped me put the trailer back on the truck.

Later when I told the Operations Director Bruce about the event, he also chuckled a bit and then told me, "That happened a few years back, but that time there was a boat still on the trailer." Instead of scolding me, he told me one of his classic stories from camp lore about a challenging, and now humorous situation where a camp staff member had created a problem, and he had worked with them to solve it. We both knew I had made a mistake, though there was some debate amongst the waterfront staff regarding who had actually hooked the trailer onto the truck. He offered grace and mentored me in how to avoid this happening again in the future.

I can also remember a time when the anchor system on one of the docks broke and needed to be repaired. The water was cold. It was windy. It had already been a long day. When I went to Bruce's office and told him what was happening, he sat back in his chair for a moment, acknowledged that the situation sounded tough, and then gave me some advice on how to address the problem. He didn't bail me out. Instead, he gave me advice on how to fix it myself and showed his confidence in me being able to get the job done. He gave me the opportunity to do the hard thing, but with guidance based on his years of experience. The problem wasn't taken from me, but I wasn't left to face it alone.

The camp experience was pivotal in helping me establish my identity and life direction. I met my wife at camp. I decided to pursue youth/young adult ministry at camp. I learned to persevere and do hard things at camp. In the camp community (shameless plug for camp ministry) young adults are valued and put into positions of responsibility. They are then mentored as they work and share the gospel with their campers. There are honest conversations regarding life and faith. Camps don't do this perfectly, and my current position at Camp MiVoden was created to try to maximize these opportunities.

However, research done a few years ago with our camping organization indicated that 83% of camp staff alumni went on to work for the church at some point in their life journey. If we compare that to a statistic where two thirds of young adults leave their church within one year of graduating high school, the contrast is stark. Being in a community that allowed them to make decisions, included them in the creative process, and then mentored them as they moved forward had a profound effect on their later involvement in their next faith community.

Church

But what about church communities? Camp is a different world that creates opportunities not available in "normal life." What does it look like for "normal" people in a "normal" community?

For Jamie, it looks like stick dramas. Jamie is in her 60s and is married to a retired schoolteacher. A number of years ago she saw a video where a youth group combined a Christian song with choreographed stick movements that embodied the song lyrics. The actors and actresses all wore black and then used their white sticks to create shapes and various motions to help tell the story. It moved her and she decided she wanted to be involved in this sort of ministry. She invited the kids in her local church to be a part of it and they began practicing. However, her involvement went beyond teaching choreography. As they learned to move together, she taught them about life together and how their participation would help spread the Gospel. She also talked to them about their lives and listened to their stories each week at practice. One performance turned into many, and she has used this ministry as a means of connecting numerous kids to a number of churches that she has been a part of.

For Jon, it looks like cooking food in the youth room. He is a bona fide foodie through and through. He is my go-to source for information regarding local food trucks and restaurants. This past year he began volunteering with the youth group in his church and soon after began cooking them breakfast. It isn't always fancy, but he enjoys connecting with the teens and sharing his love for cuisine of all kinds. He listens to stories, tells a few of his own, and plans lake events during the summer. "Someone took me out water skiing when I was a teen" he explained, "and I want to make sure our youth group has that opportunity as well."

At my church it is multifaceted. We are working on starting an initiative called Mission Z. (Cheesy name acknowledged) The idea is to recruit "covert operatives" in older generations to begin connecting with teens and young adults at church by engaging them and listening to their stories. I am booking appointments to meet with older generations in their small groups, seeking out one-on-one conversations, and using any other means I can think of (e.g. writing a book) to create opportunities to teach people about their own identity and how to show others they are valuable. For those who are willing to accept the mission, we are developing training materials and plan to maintain monthly communication to encourage them. Our goal is to create a community full of people who are looking for opportunities to engage others with the intent of helping them experience the Gospel. (a.k.a. showing them their value as children of God) We are working through our men's ministry Forged, to encourage personal spiritual growth and address the shame and guilt that keeps us focused on ourselves. There are others focused on spreading love and grace in other parts of our church ministry.

What does it look like for you and your faith community? I don't know. Maybe you love to mountain bike and invite others to join you, using your hobby as a means of connecting with teens and young adults. Maybe when you are driving, unloading bikes, or resting you have the opportunity to listen to their story. Maybe you play music and begin mentoring some young musicians. As you help them understand the rhythms and dynamics of the music, you also have a chance to listen as they describe the rhythms and dynamics in their lives. Or perhaps you love to cook, and you invite a group of young adults to join you as you create and then test your creations. (This one is a pretty safe bet. Young adults are always hungry.) Another approach is to look for opportunities to serve your local community and invite younger generations to join you. Serving others creates excellent opportunities to connect cross-generationally.

Here's what I do know. If we can create a movement where people begin to experience love and grace in their own lives, and then provide them with tools to help spread that love and grace to others, our families, churches, schools, towns, and cities will never be the same. It will look different in each community, and it should. We all have a different story. But when we start to understand what it truly means to be a child of God, we begin to see the world differently and we become a new creation. A church full of such creations can change the world. This is the way forward. I hope you'll join me in walking it.

Points to Ponder

1. What are some of the ways you have seen Christians struggle to not be "kooks?" What are some of the ways that you struggle with this?

2. Do you feel like you have ever heard God speak? What happened?

3. What do you do to create time and space in your own life to hear God speak?

4. What do you think would be different about your faith community if we were more intentional about creating

time and space for the Holy Spirit to communicate with us?

5. What can you do to help your faith community be a place where teens and young adults are welcomed and valued? What can you do to help older generations feel welcomed and valued?

JOIN THE MOVEMENT

I hope that reading *A Way Forward* has inspired you to action. The only way we span the gap is by adding more bridge builders. I may not have all the answers for your situation, but I think I know some of the right questions. Whether you're processing what this might look like in your faith community, celebrating your wins, or need a bit of encouragement I'd love to continue the conversation. Add your voice and join the movement on social media. Invite your friends to join as well. If you found this book helpful, pass it on to a friend. Are you interested in having me come and process these ideas with you and your faith community? Let's talk. Together I really do believe we can bring about change.

Email: awayforwardministries@gmail.com

Instagram: www.instagram.com/awayforwardministries

Facebook: www.facebook.com/a.way.forward.ministries.com munity

ACKNOWLEDGEMENTS

There are many people who have been a part of my life journey and helped shape my path in ministry. I am so thankful for my wife Calista who has supported my endeavors, celebrated my wins, encouraged me when the circumstances were difficult, and challenged me to grow through the process. She is the love of my life, and I'm so thankful to have her as my partner. My kids Reef and Emery have instilled joy and created many opportunities for learning in my life. I'm so proud of both of them and thankful for the opportunity to be a part of their journey into adulthood. My parents Randy and Jamie, as well as my brothers Jeremy and Ezra, have helped me process my ideas and endured years of ministerial rants and unsolicited advice. Aunt Bette believed in my ministry and helped make this project possible.

In addition to my family there are many who have helped me along the way. Dennis Ray and Sam McKee helped guide me through my first years as a pastor. Ron and Barbara Hessel gave me a new understanding of grace and created a ministry environment that facilitated growth and healing. Ashley Silva has been an incredible friend and partner in multiple facets of ministry. Additionally Jeff Wines, Jorge Jimenez, Barclay Henry, Ashley Silva and Denise Kinney are an incredible team that I am honored to be a part of at Camp MiVoden. My editor Geoff Heald has challenged me to grow in my writing and has helped me process ideas.

In addition to those I have mentioned, there are many others who have influenced me, supported me, and offered me grace. I am so thankful for the community I am blessed to be a part of.

ABOUT THE AUTHOR

Caleb Foss spent sixteen years as a youth and young adult pastor before becoming the Director of Programming and Staff Mentorship at Camp MiVoden in Hayden, Idaho. His education includes a Bachelor's Degree in Theology from Walla Walla University and a Doctorate of Physical Therapy from Eastern Washington University. He is married and has two children, along with two dogs, three cats, four chickens, a hamster and a bunny. When not at camp, he and his family can typically be found chasing powder in the mountains, relaxing on a lake or surfing in the Pacific Ocean.

ENDNOTES

The Exodus

1. Earls, Aaron. "Most Teenagers Drop Out of Church When They Become Young Adults," Lifeway Research, Lifeway, 2019. https://research.lifeway.com/2019/01/15/most-teenagers-drop-out-of-church-as-young-adults/

2. ibid

3. ibid

4. Ratcliffe, Susan. "Oxford Essential Quotations (4 ed.)" Oxford Reference, Oxford University Press, 2016. https://www.oxfordreference.com/view/10.1093/acref/9780191826719.001.0001/q-oro-ed4-00011516

5. Wallace, J Warner. "UPDATED: Are Young People Really Leaving Christianity?" Cold Case Christianity, 2019. https://coldcasechristianity.com/writings/are-young-people-really-leaving-christianity/

6. Pickett, Candace Coppinger, Justin L. Barrett, Cynthia B. Eriksson, and Christina Kabiri. "Social Networks among Ministry Relationships: Relational Capacity, Burnout, & Ministry Effectiveness." Journal of Psychology and Theology 45 (2) 2018: 92–105.

7. Roose, Caleb. "Relational Capacity and Ministry Burnout", (Blog), Fuller Youth Institute, July 19, 2018. https://fulleryouthinstitute.org/blog/relational-capacity

8. Earls, Aaron. "Most Teenagers Drop Out of Church When They Become Young Adults," Lifeway Research, Lifeway, 2019. https://research.lifeway.com/2019/01/1 5/most-teenagers-drop-out-of-church-as-young-adults/

Adolescent Abandonment

1. Clark, Chap, "Ministry in an age of delayed adulthood", (Blog), Fuller Youth Institute, September 7, 2005. https://fulleryouthinstitute.org/blog/youth-mini stry-in-an-age-of-delayed-adulthood

2. Powell, Kara, Griffen, Brad M. 3 Big Questions that Change Every Teenager, Baker Publishing Group, 2021.

3. Handwerk, Brian, "Puberty Is Beginning Earlier in Girls, So What Can Parents Do?", Science, Smithsonian Magazine, December 26, 2014. https://www.smithsonianmag.com/science-nature/puberty-beginning-earlier-girls-so-what-can-parents-do-180953738/

4. Sole-Smith, Virginia, "Why Are Girls Getting Their Periods So Young?", Fitness, Scientific American, May 1, 2019. https://www.scientificamerican.com/article/why-are-girls-getting-their-periods-so-young/

5. Eckert-Lind, Camilla, Busch, Alexander S., Petersen, Jorgen H., "Worldwide Secular Trends in Ag at Pubertal Onset Assessed by Breast Development Among Girls", JAMA Pediatr. 2020;174(4):e195881. https://jamanetwork.com/journals/jamapediatrics/fullarticle/2760573

6. Vo, Lam Thuy, "Child Labor in America: 1920", Planet Money, NPR, August 17, 2021. https://www.npr.org/sections/money/2012/08/16/158925367/child-labor-in-america-1920

7. Leon, Carol Boyd, "The Life of American Workers in 1915", Monthly Labor Review, August, 2015. https://www.bls.gov/opub/mlr/2016/article/the-life-of-american-workers-in-1915.htm

8. Cohn, D'Vera, Passel, Jeffrey S., Wang, Wendy, Livingston, Gretchen, "Barely Half of U.S. Adults Are Married – A Record Low", Pew Research Center, December 14, 2011. https://www.pewresearch.org/social-trends/2011/12/14/barely-half-of-u-s-adults-are-married-a-record-low/

9. Julian, Christopher A., "Median Age at First Marriage, 2021", Family Profile No. 15, Bowling Green State University, 2021. https://www.bgsu.edu/ncfmr/resources/data/family-profiles/julian-median-age-first-marriage-2021-fp-22-15.html

10. Sawyer, Susan M et al. "The age of adolescence." The Lancet. Child & adolescent health vol. 2,3 (2018): 223-228. doi:10.1016/S2352-4642(18)30022-1

11. Kara Powel, Jake Mulder, Brad Griffin, Growing Young: Six Essential Strategies to Help Young People Discover and Love Your Church, Baker Publishing Group, 2016, Pg 100-102

12. National Center for Health Statistics. U.S. Census Bureau, Household Pulse Survey, 2020–2023. Anxiety and Depression. Generated interactively: from https://www.cdc.gov/nchs/covid19/pulse/mental-health.htm

13. Maria A. Villarroel, Ph.D., and Emily P. Terlizzi, M.P.H., "Symptoms of Depression Among Adults: United States, 2019", NCHS Data Brief, no 379. Center for Disease Control and Prevention, September 2020. https://www.cdc.gov/nchs/products/databriefs/db379.htm

14. Renée Peltz Dennison Ph.D., "Do Half of All Marriages Really End in Divorce?", Heart of the Matter, Psychology Today, April 24, 2017. https://www.psychologytoday.com/us/blog/heart-the-matter/201704/do-half-all-marriages-really-end-in-divorce.

15. National Coalition Against Domestic Violence, "Domestic Violence", NCADV, 2020. https://ncadv.org/STATISTICS

16. Ryan Jenkins, "3 Things Making Gen Z they Loneliest Generation" Psychology Today, August 16, 2022. https://www.psychologytoday.com/us/blog/the-case-connection/202208/3-things-making-gen-z-the-loneliest-generation

17. ibid

18. ibid

The Identity Problem

1. You can listen to the audio of this interview here. https://freakonomics.com/podcast/abortion-and-crime-revisited/

2. Donohue, John J, Levitt, Steven D., "The Impact of Legalized Abortion on Crime Over the Last Two Decades", Becker Friedman Institute for Economics at UChicago, May 2019. https://bfi.uchicago.edu/wp-content/uploads/BFI_WP_201975.pdf

3. Donohue, John J, Levitt, Steven D., "The Impact of Legalized Abortion on Crime Over the Last Two Decades", The Quarterly Journal of Economics, Vol. CXVI, Issue 2, May 2001. http://pricetheory.uchicago.edu/levitt/Papers/DonohueLevittTheImpactOfLegalized2001.pdf

Understanding Our Own Identity

1. "Grace." Merriam-Webster.com Dictionary, Merriam-Webster, https://www.merriam-webster.com/dictionary/grace

2. Yancey, Philip, What's So Amazing About Grace?, Zondervan, September 9, 2008

3. ibid

4. Liversidge, Bill, Victory in Jesus, Creative Growth Ministries, January 1, 2007

Understanding the Identity of Others

1. Boardman, Madeline, "10 of the most valuable Antiques Roadshow finds", Entertainment Weekly, July 19, 2022. https://ew.com/tv/antiques-roadshow-most-valuable/

Mind the Gap

1. Pew Research Center, "They Generation Gap in American Politics," Pew Research Center Report, March 1, 2018. https://www.pewresearch.org/politics/2018/03/01/the-generation-gap-in-american-politics/

2. Ibid.

3. Ibid.

The Importance of Older Generations

1. A study from a few years back indicated that approximately 83% of summer camp staff in our camp system go on to be employed by a church at some point in their life journey.

A Way Forward

1. Ibid.

Mentoring 101

1. Top 35 Pete Carroll Quotes (2023 Update), QuoteFancy, 2023. https://quotefancy.com/pete-carroll-quotes

2. ibid

3. ibid

4. Celebrity Beliefs, Pete Carroll, Celebrity Beliefs, 2016. http://www.celebritybeliefs.com/pete-carroll/

5. Comer, John Mark, The Ruthless Elimination of Hurry, Waterbrook, 2019

The Final Ingredient

1. Reed, Betsy, "Fake doctor who worked in NHS for 20 years found guilty of fraud." Crime, The Guardian, Feb 15, 20234. https://www.theguardian.com/uk-news/2023/feb/15/fake-doctor-zholia-alemi-nhs-guilty-fraud

2. Walker, Amy, "Zholia Alemi: How the bogus psychiatrist who stole over a MILLION from the NHS went undetected for so long." Manchester Evening News, Feb 28, 2023. https://www.manchestereveningnews.co.uk/news/greater-manchester-news/zholia-alemi-how-bogus-psychiatrist-26356059

3. Merriam-Webster, "The Origin of 'Hypocrite'". Word History, https://www.merriam-webster.com/words-at-play/hypocrite-meaning-origin